EMILE DURKHEIM

Masters of Social Theory
Volume 2

MASTERS OF SOCIAL THEORY

Series Editor:

Jonathan H. Turner, *University of California, Riverside*

This new series of short volumes presents prominent social theorists of the nineteenth and twentieth centuries. Current theory in sociology involves analysis of these early thinkers' work, which attests to their enduring significance. However, secondary analysis of their work is often hurried in larger undergraduate texts or presented in long scholarly portraits.

Our attempt is to provide scholarly analysis and also to summarize the basic, core idea of the individual master. Our goal is to offer both a short scholarly reference work and individual texts for undergraduate and graduate students.

In this series:

Forthcoming volumes and their authors include the following:

EMILE DURKHEIM

An Introduction to
Four Major Works

Robert Alun Jones

Masters of Social Theory
Volume 2

Cover Photo: Encyclopaedia Britannica, *1974,*
Courtesy of Presses Universitaires de France

SAGE PUBLICATIONS
The Publishers of Professional Social Science
Beverly Hills   London   New Delhi

For information address:

SAGE Publications, Inc.
275 South Beverly Drive
Beverly Hills, California 90212

SAGE Publications India Pvt. Ltd.
M-32 Market
Greater Kailash I
New Delhi 110 048 India

SAGE Publications Ltd
28 Banner Street
London EC1Y 8QE
England

Printed in the United States of America

Library of Congress Cataloging-in-Publication Data

Jones, Robert Alun
    Emile Durkheim: an introduction to four major works.

    (Masters of social theory; v. 2)
    Bibliography: p.
    1. Durkheim, Emile, 1858-1917.   2. Durkheimian school
of sociology.   I. Title.   II. Series.
HM22.F8D828   1985   301'.01   85–18433
ISBN 0–8039–2333–3
ISBN 0–8039–2334–1 (pbk.)

FIRST PRINTING

CONTENTS

When reading the works of an important thinker, look first for the apparent absurdities in the text and ask yourself how a sensible person could have written them. When you find an answer . . . when those passages make sense, then you may find that more central passages, ones you previously thought you understood, have changed their meaning.

T. S. Kuhn, *The Essential Tension*

Editor's Introduction

In this second volume of the Sage Masters of Social Theory series, Robert Alun Jones provides a detailed summary of Emile Durkheim's four most important works—*The Division of Labor in Society, The Rules of the Sociological Method, Suicide,* and *The Elementary Forms of the Religious Life.* These works constitute the core of Durkheim's sociological thought; and thus, it is appropriate that these are highlighted. But Jones does more; he also weaves into his discussion the relevant portions of Durkheim's less well known works. The end result is one of the most complete and insightful summaries of Durkheim's thought.

R. A. Jones is well known for his advocacy of the "historicist" position—that is, the examination of historical works in terms of the issues and debates of their own time. He has consistently argued against the "presentist" position of analyzing classic works with reference to the intellectual problems of today. For as he emphasizes, the questions and debates, as well as the personalities and intellectual politics, of a time change; and it is unfair and inappropriate to impose our present-day criteria on scholars of the past. It is for this reason that Jones has examined the texts themselves, providing summaries and extensive footnotes. Only in a separate section at the end of each chapter does Jones offer some "presentist" remarks. But even here, he is cautious and unwilling to engage in the elaborate critiques, reconstructions, and reinterpretations of the classics so typical of social theory today.

Why read the early masters, especially if we are not going to examine them in terms of their contemporary relevance? Jones answer is that these masters were great sociological thinkers and understanding how they thought is, per se, an important task. By seeing how great masters dealt with the issues and problems of their times can broaden our own perspective and can, as Jones concludes, alert us to the "almost limitless possibilities of the sociological imagination."

I do not fully agree with Jones here, being a rather confirmed "presentist." But I think that the reader of these pages will come to appreciate what can be done with this more historical orientation. For in what is designed to be a short book, Jones has summarized and placed into intellectual context the corpus of Durkheim's thought. This book is by far the best review of Durkheim's work and should become a basic reference text for scholars of all intellectual persuasions—whether hopeless "presentists" like me or more historically inclined scholars.

Jonathan H. Turner

Preface

The reader of a short introductory work on Durkheim might reasonably expect three things. The first is a relatively accurate account of what Durkheim said and did—of the actions he performed, including the beliefs and intentions which characterized them. This was my first concern in the five chapters which follow. Because these actions were extremely complex, however, and because this book is intended primarily for an audience reading Durkheim (or even about Durkheim) for the first time, I have focused primarily on four books: *The Division of Labor in Society* (1893), *The Rules of Sociological Method* (1895), *Suicide* (1897), and *The Elementary Forms of the Religious Life* (1912). These are by no means the only works of Durkheim to capture the interest and imagination of modern sociologists; and, where appropriate, I have tried to indicate the significance of related works in the text or, more frequently, in the notes; but these are clearly Durkheim's "major" works in sociological theory, and I have been more concerned to make their content clear than to present a broader, but necessarily more superficial, survey of Durkheim's corpus. To the same end, I have tried to avoid reference to those abstractions—e.g., voluntarism, determinism, nominalism, realism, idealism, materialism, holism, positivism, sociologism, etc.—which befog so many of the pages written on classical sociological theorists. Instead, firmly committed to the belief that intellectual history is about people thinking and doing things rather than about abstractions (which, after all, are incapable of doing anything whatsoever), I have tried to provide an account which Durkheim himself might in principle have accepted as a description of what he was thinking and doing.

Second, our hypothetical reader might also ask for an account of why Durkheim said and did these things. I think of the causal explanation of complex ideas as so risky a business that I prefer not to think of it at all; but I have suppressed these preferences at least to the extent of offering a kind of "explanation-sketch," indicating what such explanations might look like if not fully arguing the causal connections thus implied. In Chapter 1, for example, I have briefly described the situation of French Jews under the Third Republic, with the obvious implication that this explains some of Durkheim's central theoretical concerns; and where these concerns surface in the text, as in Durkheim's defense of secular education in Book Two of *Suicide*, the appropriate inferences have been drawn.

Similarly, I have tried to indicate the sense in which Durkheim's theories (like all theories) were consistently the "answers" to quite specific "questions," and wherever possible—as in the early pages of the chapter on *The Division of Labor*—I have indicated what these questions were; and since (for all his personal austerity) Durkheim was no recluse, but rather lived and wrote in a most vibrant intellectual milieu, I have frequently, in the text and especially in the notes, mentioned the major antecedent and contemporaneous influences upon him. I have also emphasized that Durkheim, like ourselves, was not someone who simply held certain beliefs; more than this, he held some beliefs *because* he held other beliefs, and thus provided reasons for believing what he did. In some cases, of course, these were not the *only* reasons (their account of why Durkheim believed what he did may be incomplete); in other cases they were not *good* reasons (they sometimes provided logical foundations insufficient to the considerable weight of belief Durkheim placed upon them); and in still other cases they were not the *real* reasons (Durkheim was sometimes mistaken as to the causes for his beliefs). But they were still *Durkheim*'s reasons—or the reasons Durkheim *gave*—for believing the things he did; and as such, they remain an ineluctable part of any intellectually responsible account of Durkheim's beliefs. To use Clifford Geertz's phrase, I have tried to provide as "thick" a description of Durkheim's intentions and meanings as a thin book will allow.

Third, the reader might expect some critical assessments of the things Durkheim said and did. The danger here is that we might forget the difference between past and present, between Durkheim's intentions and our own, and thus subject him to praise or blame to precisely the extent that he succeeded or failed in the effort to become ourselves. It is such forgetfulness, of course, which history is written to overcome, and I have thus limited my "critical remarks" on each of the four works in question to those addressed to an action Durkheim might conceivably have performed. But however methodologically discreet, these limitations were hardly restrictive in practice; for Durkheim remains so close to us that it is rarely anachronistic to assume that his rationality is also ours. The remarks in question could easily have been more extensive, therefore, and are intended as suggestive rather than exhaustive.

Finally, I have avoided any lengthy discussions of Durkheim's considerable contributions to contemporary sociological theory, in part because they have been so great, and in part because so many of them—e.g., the labeling theorists' appropriation of Durkheim's views on crime—have depended upon the kind of historical misunderstanding just indicated. In either case, the burden of explication would be more than this small book will bear.

This "close reading" of the classics has only increased my admiration for Steven Luke's *Durkheim* (1972), as its frequent appearance in my notes will testify; and I owe a more general intellectual debt to Lew Coser's unrelenting support for a history of sociological theory which is genuinely historical. I am grateful to Jon Turner for inviting me to write this volume for his "Masters" series, and to Al Goodyear of Sage Publications for his assistance in its production. Joseph Fratesi read the page proofs despite an untimely illness, and Margaret Quinn and Sheila Welch exhibited all the Stoic virtues while processing the manuscript, particularly when the entire chapter on *Suicide* was lost through a "glitch" in the system. Mercifully, it reappeared as mysteriously as it had gone.

1

Between Two Wars

On July 19, 1870, on the most trivial of grounds, the irresponsible, decaying government of Napoleon III declared war on Prussia. The war was short, for Bismarck had taken care to isolate his enemy in advance. The British, alarmed by French adventures in Mexico, offered no assistance. The Italians, who had long awaited the chance to seize Rome, did so as the French withdrew their forces for use against Prussia. And the Russians, eager to upset the clause of the Peace of 1856 which forbade their navy access to the Black Sea, did so in 1870. By September 2, after the battle of Sedan, the technically backward French army had surrendered to Germany, and Napoleon III himself had been taken prisoner. Two days later, the Second Empire destroyed, Paris insurrectionaries, following the precedents of 1792 and 1848, proclaimed the Third French Republic, and sought desperately to continue the war. Paris was surrounded, besieged, and, by January, 1871, forced to capitulate.

The "peace" was as humiliating as the war. Since France possessed no government with which Bismarck could negotiate, he insisted on the election of a Constituent Assembly by universal male suffrage. But again, as in 1797 and 1848, republicanism proved unpopular, especially in rural areas. Suspected of bellicosity abroad, with instability at home, opposition to the Church, egalitarian, and even socialistic tendencies, republicans won only 200 of the more than 600 seats in the new Assembly. Bismarck then demanded an indemnity of 5 billion gold francs and the cession, to the newly formed German Empire, of the entire border region of Alsace and most of the province of Lorraine. Paris republicans, who had defended France when Napoleon III could not, refused to recognize the authority of this largely monarchist National Assembly. The result was civil war between the Assembly, now at Versailles, and the "Paris Commune," which lasted from March until its ruthless suppression in May, 1871, when the peace dictated by Bismarck was at last embodied in the treaty of Frankfurt.

Such was the birth of the Third French Republic. The shock produced by these events, wrote a brilliant French sociologist in 1900,

> was the stimulant that reanimated men's minds. The country found itself faced with the same question as at the beginning of the century. The organization, or rather the facade, which constituted the imperial system had just collapsed; it was a matter of remaking another, or rather of making one which could survive other than by administrative artifice—that is, one which was truly grounded in the nature of things. For that, it was necessary to know what this nature of things was; consequently, the urgent need for a science of societies made itself felt without delay.[1]

This sociologist, of course, was David Emile Durkheim, born on April 15, 1858, in Epinal, capital town of the department of Vosges, in Lorraine. His mother, Mélanie, was a merchant's daughter, and his father, Moïse, had been rabbi of Epinal since the 1830s, and was also Chief Rabbi of the Vosges and Haute-Marne. Emile, whose grandfather and great-grandfather had also been rabbis, thus appeared destined for the rabbinate, and a part of his early education was spent in a rabbinical school. This early ambition was dismissed while he was still a schoolboy, and soon after his arrival in Paris, Durkheim would break with Judaism altogether. But he always remained the product of a close-knit, orthodox Jewish family, as well as that long-established Jewish community of Alsace-Lorraine that had been occupied by Prussian troops in 1870, and suffered the consequent anti-Semitism of the French citizenry. Later, Durkheim would argue that the hostility of Christianity toward Judaism had created an unusual sense of solidarity among the Jews: "Their need of resisting a general hostility, the very impossibility of free communication with the rest of the population, has forced them to strict union among themselves. Consequently, each community became a small, compact and coherent society with a strong feeling of self-consciousness and unity" (1897b: 160).

---

1. Durkheim (1900:12). All citations are to Durkheim's works unless otherwise indicated.

An outstanding student at the Collège d'Epinal, Durkheim skipped two years, easily obtaining his *baccalauréats* in Letters (1874) and Sciences (1875), and distinguishing himself in the *Concours Général*. Intent now on becoming a teacher, Durkheim left Epinal for Paris to prepare for admission to the prestigious Ecole Normale Supérieure. Installed at a *pension* for non-resident students, however, he became utterly miserable: his father's illness left him anxious over his family's financial security; he was an utter *provincial* alone in Paris; and his intellectual predilections, already scientific rather than literary, were ill-fitted to the study of Latin and rhetoric essential for admission to the Ecole. After failing in his first two attempts at the entrance examination (in 1877 and 1878), Durkheim was at last admitted near the end of 1879.

Durkheim's generation at the Ecole was a particularly brilliant one, including not only the socialist Jean Jaurès, who became Durkheim's life-long friend, but also the philosophers Henri Bergson, Gustave Belot, Edmond Goblot, Felix Rauh, and Maurice Blondel, the psychologist Pierre Janet, the linguist Ferdinand Brunot, the historians Henri Berr and Camille Jullian, and the geographer Lucien Gallois. Despite constant fears of failure (which, according to Steven Lukes, accompanied him throughout his life), Durkheim became an active participant in the high-minded political and philosophical debates that characterized the Ecole; and, like Jaurès, he was soon a staunch advocate of the republican cause, with special admiration for Léon Gambetta, the brilliant orator and "spiritual embodiment" of the Third Republic, and the more moderate Jules Ferry, whose anti-clerical educational reforms would soon lead to a national system of free, compulsory, secular education.

Durkheim's concerns were less political than academic, however, and while he continued to criticize the literary rather than scientific emphasis of the Ecole, he discovered at least three scholars of a more congenial spirit. The first, though not an academic, was the neo-Kantian philosopher Charles Renouvier, whose ideas—e.g., **uncompromising rationalism, the scientific study of morality, reconciliation of natural determinism with moral freedom, anti-**utilitarianism, respect for bourgeois values, advocacy of secular, republican education, etc.— not only were a constant and increasingly valuable resource for Durkheim, but literally provided the secular ideology of the Third Republic from 1870 to 1900. The second—also a neo-Kantian philosopher—was Emile Boutroux, who agreed with

Auguste Comte that each science was irreducible to the science preceding it, and thus appears to have suggested to Durkheim that sociology must have both its own subject matter and its own principles of explanation. The third was the great French historian Numas-Denis Fustel de Coulanges, whose Cartesian denunciation of "preconceived ideas" and classic study of the influence of ancient religion on Greek and Roman social organization (see *La Cité antique*, 1864) may have influenced *The Rules of Sociological Method* (1895) and *The Elementary Forms of the Religious Life* (1912), respectively.

Though ill through much of 1881–1882, Durkheim successfully passed his *agrégation* (the competitive examination required for admission to the teaching staff of State secondary schools, or *lycées*), and began teaching philosophy in 1882. He had already decided that the subject of his principal doctoral thesis was to be the relations between "individualism" and "socialism"; but, as these "isms" imply, he saw this as involving contrasting philosophies or ideologies rather than "social facts." By 1883, however, Durkheim had defined the problem as one of the relations between the "individual" and "society" and, still later, between the "individual personality" and "social solidarity"; and by 1886 he had not only concluded that the solution to this problem belonged to "the new science of sociology," but had set about revising the methodological foundations for that science left behind by Comte. It was this interest in the scientific study of social facts which led Durkheim to Germany in 1885–1886.

Since the Franco-Prussian war, the humiliations of which were frequently blamed on the superiority of German secular education, the Ministry of Public Education in France had made a point of awarding scholarships to the brightest young *agrégés* to visit Germany and to become acquainted with recent scientific and scholarly achievements. Most of the French visitors were highly critical; but Durkheim was impressed, and wrote two articles—"La Philosophie dans les universités allemandes" and "La Science positive de la morale en Allemagne" (both published in 1887)—expressing his admiration for German philosophy and social science. In particular, Durkheim praised the "socialists of the chair" (e.g., Adolf Wagner and Gustav Schmoller) for their insistence on the social context of economic phenomena; the Germans' "organic" conception of the relationship between the individual and society; the generally Kantian philosophy, which Durkheim doubtless saw through Renouvierist eyes; and above all else, the scientific study of morality, particularly as pursued in the psychological laboratory of Wilhelm Wundt. For Wundt simultaneously recognized both the importance of independent social causes and the triviality of individual pre-meditation. The introduction of such a science of morality into the *lycées*, Durkheim thought, would create precisely that liberal, secular, republican ideology essential to the preservation of the Third Republic; and he thought it ironic that the Germans placed so much emphasis on such studies, while the French had been the first to govern themselves democratically.

In fact, an instrument for this purpose already existed. In 1882, the Faculty of Letters at Bordeaux had established France's first course in pedagogy for prospective school teachers, and in 1884 the state had begun to support it as part of its drive for a new system of secular, republican education. The course was first taught by Alfred Espinas, whose *Les Sociétés animaux* (1877) Durkheim greatly admired, but who was soon elevated to Dean of the Faculty. Durkheim's articles on German philosophy and social science had by now caught the attention of Louis Liard, then Director of Higher Education in France. A devoted republican and Renouvierist, Liard both resented the German pre-eminence in social science and was intrigued by Durkheim's suggestions for the reconstruction of a secular, scientific French morality. At the instigation of Espinas and Liard, therefore, Durkheim was appointed in 1887 as "Chargé d'un Cours de Science Sociale et de Pédagogie" at Bordeaux. The "Science Sociale" was a concession to Durkheim, and it was under this guise that sociology now officially entered the French university system.

The appointment of a young social scientist to the predominantly humanist Faculty of Letters at Bordeaux was not without opposition, and Durkheim exacerbated this by emphasizing the value of sociology to the more traditional humanist disciplines of philosophy, history, and law. He thus aroused (justifiable) fears of "sociological imperialism" (as in his life-long belief that metaphysical antinomies could be "resolved" sociologically) and unjustifiable (though under-standable) fears that his particular explanations of legal and moral institutions through reference to purely social causes undermined free will and individual moral agency. These fears, particularly as aroused by *The Division of Labor in Society* (1893), long excluded Durkheim from the powerful Paris professorship to which he aspired. Nonetheless, he gained the support and even allegiance of at least some of his Bordeaux colleagues—e.g., the legal scholar Léon Duguit, the Roman historian Jullian, the rationalist, neo-Kantian philosopher Octave Hamelin, and Georges Rodier, an expert on Aristotle. With Hamelin and Rodier, in particular, Durkheim joined to form a celebrated "trio" of rationalist opposition to those forms of mysticism and intuitionism which were increasingly denounced under the epithet *bergsonisme*.

Throughout his Bordeaux period (1887-1902), Durkheim's primary responsibility was to lecture on the theory, history, and practice of education. Each Saturday morning, however, he also taught a public lecture course on "social science," devoted to "specialized studies of particular social phenomena" (Lukes, 1972: 137); and it was in these public courses, some repeated several times in both Bordeaux and Paris, that Durkheim's major sociological ideas received their earliest expression. The first, for example, was titled "Social Solidarity," and set out the argument which later became *The Division of Labor in Society*. The second, on family and kinship, was a personal favorite of Durkheim's, and he planned a major work in the area for future years. The work was never completed, but Durkheim's interest, especially as deepened by his discovery of English and American ethnography in the late 1890s, was sufficient to produce important shorter pieces like "La Prohibition de l'inceste et ses origines" (1898) and "Sur le totémisme" (1902). The lecture course on suicide, first offered in 1889–1890, led directly to the work of that title published in 1897. Subsequent courses on crime (1892–1893), religion (1894–1895), the history of socialism (1895–1896), the sociology of law and politics (1896–1900), and the history of sociological doctrines (1901–1902) enjoyed similarly important consequences.

But during the same period, Durkheim's most fundamental sociological ideas were undergoing a significant change. Durkheim's early approach to the study of social phenomena, for example, was largely evolutionary, historical, and comparative, and focused on law and custom as the best indices of change in social structure; later, he came to recognize the importance of ethnographic data (a resource he had earlier not so much ignored as dismissed), a trend epitomized in his focus on the "crucial experiment" of Australian aboriginal religion in *The Elementary Forms of the Religious Life* (1912). Again, Durkheim's early work exhibited a naive evolutionary optimism common to many Victorian social scientists, suggesting that advanced industrial societies (after a brief period of "pathological" disorganization) would be almost mechanically self-regulating; later, in part under the delayed influence of Albert Schaeffle's *Die Quintessenz des Sozialismus* (1875), he would recognize the need for external regulation by occupational groups, and would embrace socialism, not so much for its economic or political advantages, but because of its "morally regenerative" possibilities. And again, Durkheim's early discussion of the *conscience collective* suggested that shared ideas and beliefs are derivative features of forms of social organization; later, the concept itself virtually disappeared from Durkheim's writing, to be replaced by collective *représentations*, more complex, differentiated states of a society's consciousness, which were also granted increased autonomy and independent explanatory power.

The results of this shift became immediately evident in one of Durkheim's most important achievements—i.e., the founding of *l'Année sociologique* (1898–1913), the first social science journal in France. Steven Lukes has suggested that Durkheim's intellectual virtuosity up to 1900 had in a sense contradicted one of his central arguments, namely that in modern societies, work (including intellectual work) should become more specialized, though remaining part of an organic whole. In 1896, therefore, putting aside his work on the history of socialism, Durkheim devoted himself to establishing a massive program of journalistic collaboration based upon a complex division of intellectual labor. Supported by a brilliant group of young scholars (mostly philosophers), the *Année* was to provide an annual survey of the strictly sociological literature, to provide additional information on studies in other specialized fields (e.g., history of law, history of religion, ethnography, social statistics, economics, etc.), and to publish original monographs in sociology. And while he encouraged his contributors and collaborators simply to work within the general, impersonal framework established in his *Rules of Sociological Method* (1895), there is no doubt that Durkheim, whose own inclination was anti-eclectic if not dogmatic, and who revised virtually all copy and even supervised proofs, imposed his own, powerful personality on the publication.

It is noteworthy that almost all of the contributors to the *Année*, like Durkheim himself by this time, were socialists, albeit socialists of a highly abstract, idealist, evolutionary, optimistic, and reformist character. Durkheim himself, who preferred the socialism of Jaurès to that of Karl Marx, Jules Guesde, or Georges Sorel, largely shared his disciples' ideals; but on the undeniable principle that scholars make poor politicians just as politicians make poor scholars, Durkheim was not an active participant in socialist politics, and limited his "morally regenerative" activities to efforts on behalf of a national system of secular education. In fact, Durkheim had an extremely low estimation of politics generally and, unlike his contemporary Max Weber, held that academics should abstain from involvement in political activities altogether. The notable exception here, as Lukes has observed, occurred when great social or moral questions became the substance of political debate, and above all when the ideals of the Republic itself were threatened. Then the academic should indeed enter the political arena, if only to "advise" and "educate" his contemporaries. The scholar might thus become an ideologist, but never a mere activist.

The extent of Durkheim's antipathy for politics can be seen in the fact that, through all the harrowing trials of the Third French Republic—e.g., the dissolution of the Chamber of Deputies in 1877, the crisis of Boulanger in 1886–1889, the Panama Canal Scandal of 1892, etc.—the exception noted above was enacted only twice: in the Dreyfus Affair, and in the First World War.

In 1894 Major Charles Esterhazy, a French staff officer riddled with gambling debts, began selling military secrets to the German Embassy in Paris. Searching for the culprit, French counter-intelligence settled on another staff officer, Captain Alfred Dreyfus, a Jew, whom they accused of treason. The accusation might still have been abandoned but for the public outcry raised by Edouard Drumond, a journalist and professional anti-Semite. Dreyfus was court-martialed, convicted of treason, and sent to Devil's Island for life. Soon thereafter, a new head of counter-intelligence, Colonel Picquart, re-examined the evidence and concluded that Dreyfus was innocent; but his superiors refused to reopen the case, forged additional documents to confirm Dreyfus's guilt, and exiled Picquart to Tunisia. When Dreyfus's brother discovered further evidence incriminating Esterhazy, the latter was court-martialed but acquitted. But by now "l'Affair Dreyfus" had become a public scandal. On January 13, 1898, *L'Aurore*, a left-wing newspaper edited by Georges Clemenceau, published Emile Zola's *J'Accuse*, an open letter to the president of the Republic denouncing the War Office for suppressing evidence and concealing a grave miscarriage of justice. The subsequent trial and conviction of Zola for libel divided the educated elite of Paris, and shook French society to its foundations. The Dreyfus Affair, Lewis Coser has aptly observed (1971: 158–159), "pitted the liberal anti-clerical defenders of the Republic against the Church and the army, the left-wing intellectuals against the nationalists, the Sorbonne against the traditional judiciary, and the local school teacher against the resident priest."

Durkheim, a Dreyfusard from a relatively early date, considered the Affair "un moment de la conscience humaine." Though he did not sign the *Manifesto of the Intellectuals* published in support of Zola the day after *J'Accuse* appeared, for example, he was an active member of the Ligue pour la Défense des Droits de l'Homme, a Dreyfusard group numbering more than 4,500 members whose commitments extended to anti-clericalism and even opposition to the Boer War. Again, when Ferdinand Brunetière, a literary critic, member of the Académie Française, and staunch anti-Dreyfusard, published a defense of the army and the Church against the anarchistic "individualism" of French intellectuals, Durkheim responded with "Individualism and the Intellectuals" (1898), an important, sociologically based argument that *modern* individualism, unlike that of Rousseau and Kant, was a product of society, a secular "religion" that derived from Christianity and sanctified liberalism, and pointed in the direction of socialism. And again, it was under the stimulus of the Dreyfus Affair that Durkheim and Hamelin founded at Bordeaux an association of secular, socialist, and anti-militarist university teachers and students called "La Jeunesse laïque." Indeed, it was Durkheim's active participation in the Dreyfus Affair that led to his appointment in Paris.

As Director of Primary Education at the Ministry of Public Instruction from 1879 to 1896, Ferdinand Buisson had been the man most responsible for implementing Ferry's educational reforms. Subsequently appointed to the chair in the Science of Education at the Sorbonne, Buisson was elected to the Chamber of Deputies in 1902, and the chair became vacant. The successful resolution of the Dreyfus Affair (Dreyfus had been pardoned in 1899 and was to be fully exonerated in 1906) had left both sociology and socialism with a more respectable public image; and Durkheim, while arguing that his competence in education was limited, and that his candidacy would thus give the appearance of using any expediency to insinuate himself in Paris, nonetheless allowed his name to go forward. After seeking letters from Boutroux, Buisson, and Victor Brochard, the Council of the Faculty of Letters at the Sorbonne appointed Durkheim *chargé d'un cours* by a large majority. Four years later Durkheim was made *professeur* by a unanimous vote and assumed Buisson's chair, which was to be renamed "Science of Education and Sociology" in 1913.

Durkheim arrived in Paris with a reputation as a powerful intellect pursuing an aggressively scientific approach to all problems (everything else was mysticism, dilettantism, and irrationalism). His "science of morality" offended philosophers, his "science of religion" offended Catholics, and his appointment to the Sorbonne (which, in the wake of the Dreyfus Affair, appeared not above extra-academic considerations) offended those on the political Right. The appointment also gave Durkheim enormous power. His lecture courses were the only required courses at the Sorbonne, obligatory for all students seeking degrees in philosophy, history, literature, and languages; in addition, he was responsible for the education of successive generations of French school teachers, in whom he instilled all the fervour of his secular, rationalist morality. As an administrator, he sat on the Council of the University as well as on many other councils and committees throughout the University and the Ministry of Public Instruction and though largely averse to politics, he numbered many powerful politicians among his personal friends. Not surprisingly, Durkheim's enemies complained of his power, accusing him of "managing" appointments and creating chairs of sociology in provincial universities in order to extend his influence. Frequently described as a "secular pope," Durkheim was viewed by critics as an agent of government anti-clericalism, and charged with seeking "a unique and pernicious domination over the minds of the young" (Lukes, 1972: 375).

Much of the hostility thus generated was the consequence of a single compulsory education course, established by Liard as part of the theoretical training of secondary school teachers, and taught by Durkheim at the Ecole Normale Supérieure each year from 1904 to 1913. As always, Durkheim took his responsibilities in education seriously, and sought to give prospective teachers a "full consciousness" of their important social function by approaching the subject historically.[2] But again, Durkheim's primary concern during his Paris years was with the sociology of morality, knowledge, and religion.

Durkheim's interest in the sociology of morality dated from his

2. Cf. *The Evolution of Educational Thought* (1938).

visit to Germany (1885–1886); and though his earliest conception of moral rules emphasized their external, obligatory character, this gradually shifted to an emphasis on the desirable, "eudaemonic" quality of moral actions, largely in the context of the course on moral education which Durkheim taught repeatedly, both in Bordeaux and Paris, between 1889 and 1912.[3] The development and deepening of this interest can be traced in both *The Division of Labor* (1893) and *Suicide* (1897); but Durkheim planned to recast these earlier views on morality in a major work entitled *La Morale*. Unfortunately, this went no further than a theoretical introduction, written in the last weeks of Durkheim's life and published three years later; but a sense of its projected content, which relies on a Kantian, "dualistic" conception of human nature, can be gathered from "The Determination of the Moral Fact" (1906), "Judgements of Value and Judgements of Reality" (1911), and the discussion of morality in *The Elementary Forms of the Religious Life* (1912).

The same dualistic conception of human nature guided Durkheim's sociology of knowledge; thus, where his sociology of morality explored the distinction between sensual appetites and moral rules, his treatment of knowledge distinguished sensations from concepts— both distinctions, of course, reflecting the more basic, all-pervasive dichotomy of the individual and society. Durkheim's attraction for these distinctions derived from the early influence of Renouvier and the later, more specifically epistemological, work of Hamelin; but in epistemology, as in ethics, Durkheim found both the Kantian and neo-Kantian solutions to the problem of knowledge unacceptable. Durkheim's own solution, relying heavily on his discovery of English and American ethnography in the late 1890s, was that society is the source of the very categories of the human reason, a stunning claim first advanced in *Primitive Classification* (1903) and extended, again, in *The Elementary Forms*.

Of all Durkheim's works, however, none has afforded such sheer intellectual excitement as *The Elementary Forms of the Religious Life*. This is all the more remarkable in light of the fact that, as Durkheim himself later admitted, his earlier treatment of religion was relatively mechanical and unimaginative. Responding in 1907 to the charge of the Catholic priest Simon Deploige that his thought was German in origin, Durkheim insisted, on the contrary, that

3. Cf. *Moral Education* (1925).

it was not until 1895 that I achieved a clear view of the essential role
played by religion in social life. It was in that year that, for the first
time, I found the means of tackling the study of religion sociologically.
This was a revelation to me. That course of 1895 marked a dividing line
in the development of my thought, to such an extent that all my
previous researches had to be taken up fresh in order to be made to
harmonize with these new insights.... This re-orientation was entirely
due to the studies of religious history which I had just undertaken, and
notably to the reading of the works of Robertson Smith and his school.
(Lukes 1972: 237)

Durkheim attempted a provisional statement of these new insights in
"On the Definition of Religious Phenomena" (1899); but he had not
yet had the opportunity fully to digest the growing body of
ethnography on primitive religions, and especially the important
accounts of Australian aborigines published by Baldwin Spencer and
F.J. Gillen in 1899 and 1904. When these data were combined with
the seminal ideas of Robertson Smith's *Religion of the Semites* (1899)
and Durkheim's own Kantian and neo-Kantian preconceptions, the
result was *The Elementary Forms*—a work which, by any standard,
remains a "classic" in the history of sociological thought.

The last course of lectures Durkheim offered before the war also
stemmed from a question raised, but not answered, in *The
Elementary Forms*—i.e., if, as Durkheim at least seemed to imply, *all*
religions are "true in their own fashion," is truth itself "relative" to
human interests and purposes? This question acquired a particular
urgency in light of the affirmative answer given to it by William
James, the increasing interest in James's pragmatism in France, and
the use of James's works as a philosophical rationale for what
Durkheim considered the anti-intellectualism of the time. Durkheim
thus presented a series of lectures in 1913–1914 which dealt not only
with James but with the elaboration of James's ideas by the Oxford
philosopher F.C.S. Schiller, their refinement by John Dewey (whom
Durkheim greatly admired), and their extension in the works of
Durkheim's life-long rival, Bergson.[4]

On August 3, 1914, Germany launched its invasion of Belgium and
northern France. All went as in the summer of 1870 until the
surprising Russians attacked East Prussia, forcing Moltke to with-
draw troops for use on the eastern front. The French army under

4. Cf. *Pragmatism and Sociology* (1955).

Joffre regrouped with support from the British, and at the battle of the Marne, fought from September 5 to 12, forced the Germans to retreat, and thus altered the entire character of the war.

Durkheim's response was one of optimism and enthusiasm. Despite poor health already induced by overwork, he devoted himself to the cause of national defense, organizing a committee for publication of studies and documents on the war, to be sent to neutral countries in the effort to undermine German propaganda. Two of the pamphlets—*Qui a voulu la guerre?* and *L'Allemagne au-dessus de tout*—were written by Durkheim himself, as were some of the patriotic pamphlets published under the title *Lettres á tous les Francais*, also organized by Durkheim and sent to his fellow-countrymen in the effort to maintain national morale. For the most part, however, Durkheim was unaffected by the war hysteria, and, though always a patriot, was never a nationalist. Indeed, by 1916 he was concerned lest a German military defeat be turned to the advantage of the conservative, "clerical" party in France; and on at least two occasions, as a native of Alsace-Lorraine and as a Jew with a German name, Durkheim suffered aspersions of disloyalty motivated by the most vulgar kind of anti-Semitism.

The greatest blow, however, was yet to come. Durkheim was utterly devoted to his son André, a linguist who had gained his *agrégation* just before the war, and was among the most brilliant of the younger *Année* circle. Sent to the Bulgarian front late in 1915, André was declared missing in January, and in April, 1916, was confirmed dead. Durkheim was devastated, withdrawing into a "ferocious silence" and forbidding friends to even mention his son's name in his presence. Burying himself all the more in the war effort, he collapsed from a stroke after speaking passionately at one of his innumerable committee meetings. After resting for several months, relieved by America's entry into the war, he recovered sufficiently to again take up his work on *La Morale*; but on November 15, 1917, he died at the age of 59.

2

The Moral Basis of the Social Order: The Division of Labor in Society (1893)

DURKHEIM'S PROBLEM

In 1776, Adam Smith opened *The Wealth of Nations* with the observation that "the greatest improvements in the productive powers of labour, and the greatest part of the skill, dexterity, and judgement with which it is anywhere directed, or applied, seem to have been the effects of the division of labour" (Smith, 1776: 3). Despite the numerous economic advantages thus derived, however, Smith insisted that the division of labor was not itself the effect of any human wisdom or foresight; rather, it was the necessary, albeit very slow and gradual, consequence of a certain propensity in human nature—"the propensity to truck, barter, and exchange one thing for another" (Smith, 1776: 13). Common to all men, this propensity could be found in no other animals; and, subsequently encouraged by the recognition of individual self-interest, it gave rise to differences among men more extensive, more important, and ultimately more useful than those implied by their natural endowments.

More than a century later, Durkheim could observe, apparently without exaggeration, that economists upheld the division of labor not only as necessary, but as "the supreme law of human societies and the condition of their progress" (1893: 39). Greater concentrations of productive forces and capital investment seemed to lead modern industry, business, and agriculture toward greater separation and specialization of occupations, and even a greater interdependence among the products themselves. And like Smith, Durkheim recognized that this extended beyond the economic world, embracing not only political, administrative, and judicial activities, but aesthetic and scientific activities as well. Even philosophy had been broken into a multitude of special disciplines, each of which had its own object, method, and ideas.

Unlike Smith, however, Durkheim viewed this "law" of the division of labor as applying not only to human societies, but to biological organisms generally. Citing recent speculation in the "philosophy of biology" (see the works of C.F. Wolff, K.E. von Baer, and H. Milne-Edwards), Durkheim noted the apparent correlation between the functional specialization of the parts of an organism and the extent of that organism's evolutionary development, suggesting that this extended the scope of the division of labor so as to make its origins contemporaneous with the origins of life itself. This, of course, eliminated any "propensity in human nature" as its possible cause, and implied that its conditions must be found in the essential properties of all organized matter. The division of labor in society was thus no more than a particular form of a process of extreme generality.

But if the division of labor was thus a natural law, then (like all natural laws) it raised certain moral questions. Are we to yield to it, or resist it? Is it our duty to become thorough, complete, self-sufficient human beings? Or are we to be but parts of a whole, organs of an organism? In other words, is this *natural law* also a *moral rule*? If so, why, and in what degree? In Durkheim's opinion, the answers of modern societies to these and similar questions had been deeply ambivalent—i.e., on the one hand, the division of labor seemed to be increasingly viewed as a moral rule, so that, in at least one of its aspects, the "categorical imperative" of the modern conscience had become: "Make yourself usefully fulfill a determinate function" (1893: 43); on the other hand, quite aside from such maxims endorsing specialization, there were other maxims, no less prevalent, which called attention to the dangers of *over*-specialization, and encouraged all men to realize similar ideals. The situation was thus one of moral conflict or antagonism, and it was this which Durkheim sought first to explain and then to resolve.

This in turn calls for two final observations. First, the method of this explanation and resolution was to be that of the so-called "science of ethics"; for Durkheim was convinced that moral facts like the division of labor were themselves natural phenomena—they consisted of certain rules of action imperatively imposed upon conduct, which could be recognized, observed, described, classified, and explained. Second, this explanation itself was but a preliminary step to the solution of practical social problems; for Durkheim always conceived of societies as subject to conditions of moral "health" or "illness," and the sociologist as a kind of "physician" who scientifically determined the particular condition of a particular society at a particular time, and then prescribed the social "medicine" necessary to the maintenance or recovery of well-being.

Durkheim's problem thus defined, his solution fell quite naturally into three principal parts: (1) the determination of the function of the division of labor; (2) the determination of the causes on which it depended; and (3) the determination of those forms of "illness" which it exhibited.

THE FUNCTION OF THE DIVISION OF LABOR

The word "function," Durkheim observed, can be used in two, quite different, senses: (1) to refer to a system of vital movements (e.g., digestion, respiration, etc.) without reference to the consequences of these movements; or (2) to refer to the relationship between these movements and the corresponding needs of the organism (e.g., digestion incorporates food essential to replenish nutritional resources of the body, while respiration introduces the necessary gases into the body's tissues; etc.). Durkheim insisted on the second usage; thus, to ask "what is the 'function' of the division of labor?" was simply to ask for the organic need which the division of labor supplied.

But at first sight, the answer to this question seemed all too clear; for, as Smith had already observed, the division of labor improves both the skill of the worker and the productive power of society, and thus its "function" would simply be to produce and secure those economic, artistic, and scientific advantages subsumed under the word "civilization." Against this, Durkheim presented two arguments. The first, which reveals Durkheim's deep, if ambivalent, debt to Rousseau, was that, if the division of labor has no other role than to render "civilization" possible, then there would be no reason to grant it the status of a "moral" fact—of rules of action imperatively imposed upon conduct. On the contrary, if the average number of crimes and suicides is employed as the "standard of morality," Durkheim argued, we must conclude that immorality increases as the economy, arts, and sciences progress. At its very best, therefore, civilization would be morally indifferent; and if its productions were the sole function of the division of labor, then it, too, would participate in this moral neutrality.

Durkheim's second argument was that, if the division of labor has no other role than to make civilization possible, then it would have no reason for existence whatsoever; for civilization, by itself, has no intrinsic value; rather, its value is derived entirely from its correspondence to certain needs. But these needs, Durkheim argued, are themselves the product of the division of labor. If the division of labor existed only to satisfy them, its only function would be to diminish needs which it itself had created. And this made little sense to Durkheim, for, while it might explain why we have to *endure* the division of labor, it would hardly be consistent with the fact that we *desire* occupational specialization and push it forward relentlessly. For the last to be intelligible, we must assume that the division of labor satisfies needs which the division of labor has not itself produced.

What, then, are these "needs" satisfied by the division of labor? As a first step toward an answer, Durkheim posed a paradox as old as Aristotle—that, while we like those who resemble us, we are also drawn toward those who are different, precisely because they *are* different. In other words, difference can be as much a source of mutual attraction as likeness. The key to resolving the paradox, Durkheim suggested, lies in recognizing that only *certain kinds* of differences attract—specifically, those which, instead of excluding one another, complement one another: "If one of two people has what the other has not, but desires, in that fact lies the point of departure for a positive attraction" (1893: 68–69). In other words, we seek in others what we lack in ourselves, and associations are formed wherever there is such a true exchange of services—in short, wherever there is a division of labor.

But if this is the case, we are led to see the division of labor in a new light[1]—the *economic* services it renders are trivial by comparison with the *moral* effect it produces. Its true function, the real need to

---

1. Durkheim acknowledged that Comte was "the first to have recognized in the division of labor something other than a purely economic phenomenon" (1893: 62).

which it corresponds, is that feeling of solidarity in two or more persons which it creates. Thus, the role of the division of labor is not simply to embellish already existing societies, but to render possible societies which, without it, would not even exist; and the societies thus created, Durkheim added, cannot resemble those determined by the attraction of like for like. Rather, they must bear the mark of their special origin.

The last point laid the immediate foundations for the next step in Durkheim's argument. Thus far, he had shown only that, in advanced societies, there is a social solidarity derived from the division of labor, something already obvious from two facts: that the division of labor does produce a kind of solidarity, and that the division of labor is highly developed in advanced societies. The question which remained was both more important and more difficult to answer: *To what degree* does the solidarity produced by the division of labor contribute to the general integration of society? This question was important because only by answering it could Durkheim determine whether this form of solidarity was essential to the stability of advanced societies, or was merely an accessory and secondary condition of that stability; and it was difficult because an answer required the systematic comparison of this form of solidarity with others, in order to determine how much credit, in the total effect, was due to each. Such a comparison in turn required a classification of the various types of solidarity to be compared, and here Durkheim faced one of the most formidable obstacles to his science of ethics: the fact that, as a "completely moral phenomenon," social solidarity did not lend itself to exact observation or measurement.

Durkheim's way of surmounting this obstacle was to substitute for this internal, moral fact an "external index" which symbolized it, and then to study the fact in light of the symbol. This external symbol was *law*—i.e., where social life exists, it tends to assume a definite, organized form, and law is simply the most stable and precise expression of this organization. Law reproduces the principal forms of solidarity; and thus we have only to classify the different types of law in order to discover the different types of solidarity corresponding to them.

This proposal encountered two immediate difficulties. The first was that some social relations are regulated not by *law*, but by *custom*; moreover, custom is frequently at odds with law, and thus may express an altogether different form of social solidarity. Here Durkheim resorted to one of his favorite (and least convincing) defenses—i.e., the distinction between the normal and the pathological. The conflict between law and custom arises where the former no longer corresponds to existing social relations, but maintains itself by habit, while the latter corresponds to these new relations, but is denied juridical expression. But such conflict, Durkheim insisted, is both rare and pathological; the normal condition is one in which custom is the very basis of law, in which custom alone can manifest only secondary forms of social solidarity, and thus in which law alone tells us which forms of social solidarity are essential. This purely arbitrary distinction, incidentally, reveals not only a profound discomfort with the ethnographic study of primitive societies, but a concerted effort to rationalize this discomfort as well.

The second objection was that social solidarity does not completely manifest itself in any perceptible form whatsoever, for law (and even custom) are but the partial, imperfect manifestations of internal psychological states which are thus the more appropriate focus for our investigations. Durkheim's response contained three interrelated arguments; first, that we can determine the nature of social solidarity scientifically only by studying its most objective and easily measurable effects (such as law); second, that, while solidarity "depends on" such internal states, these are not equivalent to social solidarity itself; and, finally, that these states themselves depend on social conditions for their explanation, a fact which explains why at least some sociological propositions find their way into the purest analyses of psychological facts.[2]

How, then, do we classify the different types of law? If the classification is to be scientific, Durkheim argued, we must do so according to some characteristic which both is essential to laws and varies as they vary. This characteristic is the *sanction*; i.e., "Every precept of law can be defined as a rule of sanctioned conduct. Moreover, it is evident that sanctions change with the gravity attributed to precepts, the place they hold in the public conscience, the role they play in society" (1893: 68–69). These sanctions, Durkheim then observed, fall into two classes: *repressive* sanctions (characteristic of penal laws), which consist in some loss or suffering inflicted on the agent, making "demands on his fortune, or on his honor, or on his life, or on his liberty, and deprive him of something he enjoys" (1893: 69); and *restitutive* sanctions (characteristic of civil,

2. Durkheim's particular reference here was to Alexander Bain's *The Emotions and the Will* (1859) and Herbert Spencer's *Principles of Psychology* (1855).

commercial, procedural, administrative, and constitutional laws), which consist "only of *the return of things as they were*, in the re-establishment of troubled relations to their normal state" (1893: 69).

The two types of law thus classified according to their characteristic sanctions, Durkheim was now in a position to determine the types of solidarity corresponding to each. The first of these Durkheim called *mechanical solidarity*—that type of solidarity characterized by repressive sanctions. And since acts calling forth such sanctions are (by definition) "crimes," then the inquiry into the nature of mechanical solidarity became an inquiry into the nature of crime.

What, then, is "crime"? While acknowledging that there are many kinds of crime, Durkheim was convinced that they all contained a common element; for otherwise the universally identical reaction to crimes (repressive sanctions) would itself be unintelligible. Nonetheless, the enormous variety of crimes suggested that this common element could not be found among the intrinsic properties of criminal acts themselves; rather, it had to be found in the relations which these acts sustain with certain external conditions. But which relations? After some characteristic annihilations of competing proposals, Durkheim concluded that the only common element in all crimes is that they shock sentiments which, "for a given social system, are found in all healthy consciences" (1893: 73). And this also explains why penal (as opposed to civil) law is "diffused" throughout the whole society rather than centralized in a special magistrate—the sentiments to which penal law corresponds are immanent in all consciousnesses.[3]

But what about acts like incest—acts which provoke widespread aversion, but are merely "immoral" rather than "criminal"? Durkheim replied that "crimes" properly so-called have an additional distinctive property not shared by simply "immoral" acts: the sentiments they offend must have a certain *average intensity*. And again, this greater intensity of sentiments responsive to crime as opposed to immoral acts is reflected in the fixity of penal law over time, by contrast with the great plasticity of moral rules. Finally, the sentiments responsive to criminal acts are also more well-defined than those nebulous sentiments evoked by immorality.

Durkheim's definition of crime thus led directly to his notion of the

3. Though Durkheim admits that penal law is often "administered" through particular magistrates.

conscience collective—"the totality of beliefs and sentiments common to the average citizens of the same society" (1893: 79)[4]—which Durkheim then endowed with quite distinctive characteristics: it forms a determinate system with its own life; it is "diffuse" in each society and lacks a "specific organ"; it is independent of the particular conditions in which individuals find themselves; it is the same in different locations, classes, and occupations; it connects successive generations rather than changing from one to another; and it is different from individual *consciences*, despite the fact that it can be realized only through them. A "crime," therefore, is simply an act which offends intense and well-defined states of this *conscience collective*, a proposition which describes not simply the "consequences" of crime, but its *essential property*: "We do not reprove it because it is a crime, but it is a crime because we reprove it" (1893: 81).[5]

But aren't there acts which do *not* offend the *conscience collective*, but which are nonetheless severely sanctioned by the state? And are there then two distinct types of crime? Durkheim insisted there are not, for the effects called forth by criminal acts are the same in either case, and the same effect must have the same cause. Durkheim was thus led to argue that the state derives its authority from the *conscience collective*, and becomes its directive organ and its symbol; but, while the state never completely frees itself from this source of its authority, it does become an autonomous, spontaneous power in social life. The extent of the state's power over the number and nature of criminal acts depends on the authority it receives from the *conscience collective*; and this authority can be measured either by the power the state exerts over its citizens, or by the gravity attached to crime against the state. As Durkheim would show, this power was greatest and this gravity most pronounced in the lowest, most primitive societies; and it was in these societies that the *conscience collective* enjoyed the greatest authority.

In effect, therefore, Durkheim argued that crime is characterized

4. The French word *conscience* embraces both the English words "conscience" and "consciousness"; thus it embraces moral and religious beliefs and sentiments, on the one hand, and cognitive beliefs and sentiments, on the other. Since translation into either English usage might create confusion, I have henceforth left this term in the original French.

5. Durkheim acknowledged the reversion of psychology to Spinoza here, as in "things are good because we like them, as against our liking them because they are good."

by its capacity to provoke punishment. But if this was the case, crime ought to explain the various characteristics of punishment, and any demonstration that it did so would augment the plausibility of Durkheim's initial argument. What, then, are the characteristics of punishment? Disregarding the conscious intentions of those applying it, Durkheim insisted that the characteristics of punishment are what they have always been—its mood is passionate; its function is vengeance, even expiation; its intensity is variable or "graduated"; its source is society rather than the individual; its cause is the violation of a moral rule; and its form is "organized" (unlike the "diffuse" repression of merely immoral acts, its implementation is the act of a definitely constituted body or tribunal). In short, punishment is "a passionate reaction of graduated intensity that society exercises through the medium of a body acting upon those of its members who have violated certain rules of conduct" (1893: 96).

How are these characteristics to be explained? Durkheim first observed that every state of *conscience* is an essential source of life, and everything that weakens such a state "wastes and corrupts" us; thus we react energetically against those ideas and sentiments which contradict our own. But the ideas and sentiments offended by crime, Durkheim argued, have particular features which in turn explain the special characteristics of punishment: i.e., because these sentiments are held with particular strength, the reaction is passionate; because these sentiments transcend individual mental states, mere restitution is unacceptable, and revenge and even expiation are called for; because the vivacity of such sentiments will nonetheless vary, the intensity of the reaction will also be variable; because such sentiments are held collectively, the source of the reaction will be society rather than the individual; and because these sentiments are well-defined, the reaction to their violation will be organized.

Having begun by establishing inductively that "crime" is an act contrary to strong and well-defined states of the *conscience collective*, therefore, Durkheim confirmed this definition by showing that crime thus defined accounts for all the characteristic features of punishment; and since the whole point of Durkheim's inquiry into the nature of crime was its promise to reveal the nature of mechanical solidarity, we might reasonably ask what has been thus revealed. Durkheim's answer was that the cause of mechanical solidarity lies in the conformity of all individual *consciences* to a common type, not only because individuals are attracted to one another through resemblance, but because each is joined to the society that they form by their union; inversely, the society is bound to those ideas and sentiments whereby its members resemble one another because that is a condition of its cohesion.

Durkheim thus introduced an idea which would assume increasing importance in his later work: the duality of human nature. Briefly, in each of us there are two *consciences*—one containing states personal to each of us, representing and constituting our individual personality; the other containing states common to all, representing society, and without which society would not exist. When our conduct is determined by the first, we act out of self-interest; but when it is determined by the second, we act morally, in the interest of society. Thus the individual, by virtue of his resemblance to other individuals, is linked to the social order. This is mechanical solidarity, which, as we have seen, is manifested through repressive law; and the greater the number of repressive laws, the greater the number of social relations regulated by this type of solidarity.

The very nature of *restitutive* sanctions, however, indicates that there is a totally different type of social solidarity which corresponds to civil law; for the restitutive sanction is not punitive, vengeful, or expiatory at all, but consists only in a return of things to their previous, normal state. Neither do violations of civil laws evoke the milder, more diffuse disapproval of merely moral transgressions; in fact, we can imagine that the laws themselves might be quite different than they are without any feeling of moral repugnance being aroused. Durkheim thus concluded that such laws, manifested in restitutive sanctions, could not derive from any strong state of the *conscience collective*, but must have some other source.

An indication of this source was afforded by an examination of the conditions under which such rules are established. Briefly, there are some relationships (typically, those involving contractual obligations) which the consent of the interested parties is not sufficient to create or to change; on the contrary, it is necessary to establish or modify such relationships juridically, by means of law. While contracts are entered and abrogated through the efforts of individuals, therefore, they have a binding, obligatory power only because they are supported and enforced by society. Most important, the contractual relations thus regulated are not "diffused" throughout the society; they do not bind the individual to society, but rather bind special parties in the society to one another.

The cooperative relations thus formed create what Durkheim called *organic solidarity*, which is derived not from the *conscience collective*, but from the division of labor. For, where mechanical solidarity presumes that individuals resemble one another, organic solidarity presumes their difference; and again, where mechanical solidarity is possible only in so far as the individual personality is submerged in the collectivity, organic solidarity becomes possible only in so far as each individual has a sphere of action peculiar to him. For organic solidarity to emerge, therefore, the *conscience collective* must leave untouched a part of the individual *conscience* so that special functions, which the *conscience collective* itself cannot tolerate, may be established there; and the more this region of the individual *conscience* is extended, the stronger is the cohesion which results from this particular kind of solidarity.

Durkheim had thus postulated two distinct types of social solidarity (mechanical and organic), each with its distinctive form of juridical rules (repressive and restitutive). In order to determine their relative importance in any given societal type, therefore, it seemed reasonable to compare the respective extent of the two kinds of rules which express or symbolize them. The preponderance of repressive rules over their restitutive counterparts, for example, ought to be just as great as the preponderance of the *conscience collective* over the division of labor; inversely, in so far as the individual personality and the specialization of tasks is developed, then the relative proportion of the two types of law ought to be reversed.

In fact, Durkheim argued, this is precisely the case. Despite the flimsy ethnographic evidence supporting such generalizations, Durkheim argued that the more primitive societies are, the more resemblances (particularly as reflected in primitive religion) there are among the individuals who compose them;[6] inversely, the more civilized a people, the more easily distinguishable its individual members.[7] Durkheim's discomfort with the ethnographic literature was still more evident when he turned to the nature of primitive law.

6. This introduced one of several disagreements between Durkheim and Gabriel Tarde. In *Les Lois de l'imitation* (1890), Tarde had suggested that civilization produces social similarities. Durkheim acknowledged the growth of similarities *between* societies and even *between* occupational types, but insisted that the individuals *within* such societies and occupations had, in fact, become progressively differentiated (cf. 1893: 137–138).

7. Here Durkheim was not above citing phrenological data provided by Gustave LeBon.

Relying on Sir John Lubbock's *Origin of Civilization* (1870) and Herbert Spencer's *Principles of Sociology* (1876–1885), he suggested that such law "appears to be entirely repressive" (1893: 138); but, insisting that such observations necessarily lack precision, Durkheim instead pointed to the evidence of written law. Moving from the Pentateuch to the "Twelve Tables" (451–450 BC) of the Romans to the laws of early Christian Europe, therefore, Durkheim argued that the relative proportions of repressive to restitutive laws are precisely those which his theory would lead us to expect.[8]

When we reach the present, therefore, we find that the number of relationships which come under repressive laws represents only a small fraction of social life; thus, we may assume that the social bonds derived from the *conscience collective* are now much less numerous than those derived from the division of labor. But one might still argue that, regardless of their number, the bonds which tie us directly to our societies through shared beliefs and sentiments have greater strength than those resulting from cooperation; and to this hypothetical objection, Durkheim had two independent answers.

First, he felt that, regardless of their undeniable rigidity, the bonds created by mechanical solidarity, even in lower societies, were inferior to those created by organic solidarity in their more advanced counterparts. Here, again, Durkheim's ethnographic resources were limited to a few passages cited from Spencer, Fustel de Coulanges, and Theodor Waitz's *Anthropologie der Naturvölker* (1859); but the source of this conviction, in any case, was less empirical than theoretical. Where, as in lower societies, the *conscience collective* is virtually coextensive with the individual *conscience*, each individual "contains within himself all that social life consists of," and thus can carry "society" wherever he wishes to go; inversely, the society, given its rudimentary division of labor, can lose any number of its members without its internal economy being disturbed. Thus, from both standpoints, the bonds connecting the individual to society based upon the *conscience collective* are less resistant to disseveration than those based upon the division of labor.

8. Durkheim acknowledged that this predominance of repressive law in ancient societies might have alternative explanations, including that presented in Henry Sumner Maine's *Ancient Law* (1861)—that reduction of law to the written word took place during a period of violence and barbarism, so that the laws were a reaction against customary behavior. Again, however, Durkheim's view of law, like his view of the state, emphasized that it *expresses* and *symbolizes* customs, reacting against them only with a force it has borrowed from them; cf. Durkheim (1893: 146).

Durkheim's second answer was that, as society evolves from a lower to a higher type, the bonds created by mechanical solidarity become still weaker. The strength of mechanical solidarity, Durkheim argued, depends on three conditions: (1) the relation between the volume of the *conscience collective* relative to the individual *conscience*; (2) the average intensity of the states of the *conscience collective*; and (3) the degree of definition of the states of the *conscience collective*. As we have seen, intense and well-defined states of the *conscience collective* are the basis of repressive laws; and, since we have also seen that the proportion of such laws has declined, it seems reasonable to assume that the average intensity and degree of definition of the *conscience collective* have also declined. The same, Durkheim admitted, cannot be said about the relative volume of the *conscience collective*; for, while that "region" of the *conscience collective* manifested by repressive laws has no doubt contracted, that region of the same *conscience* expressed through less intense and more vague sentiments of custom and public opinion may in fact have expanded. But meanwhile, Durkheim argued, the volume of the individual *conscience* has grown in at least equal proportions; for, "if there are more things common to all, there are many more that are personal to each" (1893: 153). The most we can say of the relative volume of the *conscience collective*, therefore, is that it has remained the same; for it certainly has not gained, and it may have lost. And if we could prove what we already have good reason to assume—that the *conscience collective* has become both less intense and more vague over time—then we could be sure that mechanical solidarity has become weaker over the same period.

How could such proof be provided? Not by comparing the number of repressive rules in different societal types, Durkheim emphasized, for this number alone does not vary exactly with the sentiments thus represented. Instead, Durkheim simply grouped the rules into classes corresponding to the types of sentiments aroused by their violation. The result was a list of "criminological types," whose number would necessarily correspond to the number of intense, well-defined states of the *conscience collective*: "The more numerous the latter are, the more criminal types there ought to be, and consequently, the variations of one would exactly reflect the variations of the other" (1893: 154).

The conclusion of Durkheim's investigation, of course, was that a large number of criminological types—those expressed by repressive laws governing sexual relations, domestic, and, most dramatically, religious life—had progressively disappeared over the centuries; and this in turn suggested that the states of the *conscience collective* had indeed become less intense and more vague, and that mechanical solidarity was commensurately weakened. The notable exception here, as Durkheim was careful to point out, were those states of the *conscience collective* which have the individual as their object, as in the protection of the individual's person and rights. And this, Durkheim (in effect) suggested, is indeed an exception which proves the rule; for it could become possible only if the individual personality had become far more important in the society, and thus only if the personal *conscience* of each individual had grown considerably more than the *conscience collective* itself. To this other proofs were added: the decline of religion (which, at this time, Durkheim literally defined as strong, commonly held beliefs) and the disappearance of those proverbs and adages whereby "collective thought condenses itself" (1893: 171). All conspired to make the same point: that the *conscience collective* had progressed less than the individual *conscience*, becoming less intense and distinct, and more abstract and indecisive.

Will the *conscience collective* then disappear? Durkheim thought not, at least in part because of the "notable exception" mentioned above—it not only survives, but becomes more intense and well-defined, in so far as its object is the individual: "As all the other beliefs and all the other practices take on a character less and less religious, the individual becomes the object of a sort of religion. We erect a cult on behalf of personal dignity which, as every strong cult, already has its superstitions" (1893: 172). But while it is from society that this cult gathers its force, it is not to society, but to ourselves, that it attaches us; thus Durkheim denied that it was a true social link, and repeated his argument that all such links derived from likeness have progressively weakened. If society itself is to survive, therefore, there must be some other "true social link" which replaces it; and this, of course, is organic solidarity, the product of the division of labor.

But if the way in which men are linked together has thus evolved from mechanical to organic solidarity, there should be parallel changes in the structural features of the societies themselves. What kind of social structure, therefore, might we expect to find in a society whose cohesiveness is based primarily on resemblances?

Briefly, we would expect what Durkheim called the *horde*—an absolutely homogeneous mass of indistinguishable parts, devoid of all form, arrangement, or organization. Durkheim admitted that no societies fitting this description had ever been observed; but among both the Iroquois[9] and Australian[10] tribes, he found societies made up of a number of groups of this kind. Durkheim thus gave the name *clan* to the horde which had become an element of a more extensive group, and used the term *segmental societies with a clan base* to refer to peoples thus constituted through an association of clans.

Durkheim chose the term "clan" because these groups are both *familial* (i.e., all members are regarded as "kin," most are consanguineous, and they practice collective punishment, collective responsibility, and, once private property appears, mutual inheritance) and *political* (i.e., not all members are consanguineous, some merely bear the same name; it attains dimensions much larger than any "family," and the heads of clans are the sole political authorities). Most important, however, the clan is internally homogeneous, and its solidarity is thus based on resemblances.[11] Even the clans themselves must bear certain resemblances if segmental organization is to be possible, although their differences must also be sufficient to prevent them from "losing themselves" in one another. This, then, is the social structure of mechanically solidary societies.

But there is also a social structure to which *organic* solidarity corresponds. Typically, such societies are constituted not by homogeneous segments, but by a system of different organs, each of which has a special role, and which themselves are formed of differentiated parts. These parts are also arranged differently: rather than being merely juxtaposed or mingled, they are coordinated and subordinated to one another around a central organ, which exercises a regulative action on the entire organism. Finally, the place of each individual in such societies is determined not by his name or kin-group, but by the particular occupation or social function to which he is committed.

This is what Durkheim called the *organized* societal type which,

9. Cf. Lewis Henry Morgan, *Ancient Society* (1877).

10. Cf. Lorimer Fison and A.W. Howitt, *Kamilaroi and Kurnai* (1880).

11. This led Durkheim into an extended criticism of Spencer, who agreed that social evolution begins from a state of homogeneity, but who also argued that such homogeneity was "inherently unstable." Durkheim, by contrast, emphasized the strong, coherent social life of such groups, based upon an abundance of common beliefs and practices (cf. 1893: 179).

because of its sharp differences from the *segmental* type, can advance only in so far as the latter is gradually effaced. But Durkheim was also aware of the considerable complexity of the transition from one to the other, and provided a particularly subtle account of the almost parasitical manner in which the new occupational "organs" at first utilize the old familial system (as when Levites became priests), the subsequent process whereby consanguineous ties give way to less resistant bonds based upon territorial allegiances, and, finally, the complete triumph of the fully "organized" societal type over the structural constraints of its earlier, "segmental," counterpart. As with the primitive horde, Durkheim admitted that this organized type was nowhere presently observable in its purest form; but he added that "a day will come when our whole social and political organization will have a base exclusively, or almost exclusively, occupational" (1893: 190).

Thus far, Durkheim's argument would have appeared relatively familiar to his contemporaries, for it bore an unmistakable similarity to that found in Spencer's *Principles of Sociology* (1876–1885), particularly in its emphasis on the growth of individuality with the advance of civilization. This similarity was sufficiently upsetting to Durkheim to provoke a more detailed account of his differences with Spencer. For the latter, for example, the submersion of the individual in lower societies was the result of force, an artificial suppression required by the essentially despotic, "military" type of organization appropriate to an early stage of social evolution. For Durkheim, by contrast, the effacement of the individual was the product of a societal type characterized by the complete absence of all centralized authority; military personality in lower societies was a consequence not of suppression, but of the fact that, in those societies, the "individual," as such, did not exist. Reversing Spencer's argument, therefore, Durkheim saw the emergence of despotic authority not as a step toward the effacement of the individual, but as the first step toward individualism itself, the chief being the first personality to emerge from the previously homogeneous social mass.

But there was more to this than a typical Durkheimian annihilation of an intellectually inferior opponent; for Durkheim sought to establish two important propositions. The first of these was hinted at in our earlier discussion of Durkheim's view of the state—that when we find a governmental system of great authority, we must seek its cause not in the particular situation of the governing, but in the nature of the societies governed. The second was that altruism, far from being a recent advance over man's selfish, egoistic tendencies, is found in the earliest societies; for, as we have seen, Durkheim had a dualistic conception of human nature, and thus both egoism and altruism were natural expressions of the human *conscience* at all stages of social evolution. ·

What, then, is the essential difference between lower societies and our own? Durkheim's answer was again worked out in opposition to Spencer, whose own answer again appeared quite similar. Spencer had observed, like Durkheim, that in industrial societies a cooperative form of solidarity is produced automatically as a consequence of the division of labor. But if Spencer thus recognized the true cause of social solidarity in advanced societies, Durkheim argued, he had not understood the way in which it produced its effect; and, misunderstanding this, Spencer had misunderstood the nature of the effect (i.e., social solidarity) itself.

Consider only two features of Spencer's conception of social solidarity: because industrial solidarity is produced automatically, it does not require the regulation or intervention of the state in order to produce or maintain it; and because the sphere of societal action is thus drastically reduced, the only surviving link between men is the relationship of contracts, freely entered and freely abrogated, according to the self-interest of the parties involved. Durkheim's initial response was that, if this is truly the character of societies whose solidarity is produced by the division of labor, we might with justice doubt their stability; for "self-interest" creates only the most ephemeral, superficial sort of social bond, and in fact disguises a more fundamental, albeit latent and deferred, conflict. The large and increasing volume of restitutive law, moreover, hardly suggested to Durkheim that the regulative intervention of the state in contractual relations was decreasing; on the contrary, it suggested that unregulated contracts alone were insufficient to secure equal justice for their contending parties—particularly the worker in contractual relations between labor and management. While Spencer was right to point to the increase in the number of social relationships governed by contract, he ignored the parallel increase in the number of *non*-contractual relations; but most important, he ignored the fact that, even *within* the contract, "everything is not contractual"—i.e., a contract assumes the predetermination of the rights and obligations of the contracting parties, a function performed not only by state-regulated contract law, but also through the less formal but nonetheless imperative structures of custom.

In short, Spencer did not understand the nature of social solidarity, nor did he understand the function of the division of labor. Whatever its economic advantages, the function of the division of labor was pre-eminently moral. In fact, contrasting the solidarity created by occupational specialization with the "inferior" bonds forged by its mechanical counterpart, Durkheim insisted that the moral character of society is more pronounced in the "organized" type. Precisely because the modern individual is not sufficient unto himself, for example, it is from society that he receives all that is necessary to life; thus is created his strong sentiment of personal dependence which inspires those mundane sacrifices we call "moral acts" and, in occasional, extreme cases, those acts of complete self-renunciation which Durkheim would take up in *Suicide* (1897). On its side, society learns to regard its members not as indistinguishable units that could be lost without serious disruption to its internal economy, but as irreplaceable organic parts which it cannot neglect, and towards which it has important obligations. It was the perfection of this moral function toward which all social evolution tended.

THE CAUSES OF THE DIVISION OF LABOR

Durkheim was always concerned to distinguish the causes of a social fact from its functions, and the division of labor was no exception. Indeed, he insisted, the causes of the division of labor could not possibly consist in some anticipation of its moral effects; for, as we have seen, those effects became evident only after a lengthy process of social evolution, and could hardly be foreseen. In a different sense, however, Durkheim's inquiry into causes rehearsed his earlier analysis of functions; for, just as the earlier discussion began with Durkheim's rejection of Adam Smith's argument that the function of the division of labor was the advancement of civilization, so the later discussion began with a negative assessment of that "classic" explanation, attributed to political economy in general, whereby the cause of the division of labor would be "man's unceasing desire to increase his happiness" (1893: 233).

Against this explanation, which would reduce the division of labor to purely individual and psychological causes, Durkheim launched a three-pronged attack. First, he challenged the axiom on which the explanation rests—namely, the assumption that man's desire to increase his happiness is indeed unceasing. Here Durkheim's early experience in Wundt's psychological laboratory served him well, for he was able to cite the famous law of the German experimental psychologist E.H. Weber (later quantified by Gustav Fechner) to the effect that the smallest increment in a stimulus required to produce a difference in the sensation experienced is not an absolute amount, but is rather relative to the magnitude of the stimulus in question. As a corollary to this law, Durkheim insisted that the intensity of any agreeable stimulus can increase usefully (i.e., contribute to increased pleasure) only between two extremes. An increase in monetary wealth, for example, must be of a certain size if pleasure is to be its result; inversely, a person thoroughly accustomed to large increases in wealth estimates the value of such increases accordingly, and is equally denied pleasure proportionate to the stimulus received. The increase in income experienced by the man of average wealth is thus the one most apt to produce a degree of pleasure proportionate to its cause. If the cause of the division of labor were the desire for happiness, therefore, social evolution would surely have come to a stop long ago; for the maximum happiness of which men are capable would have been achieved through a relatively moderate development of social differentiation and its resulting stimuli.[12] This insistence that the human capacity for happiness is very limited, a kind of Aristotelian ethics augmented by Wundt's *Grunzüge der physiologische Psychologie* (1874), remained one of Durkheim's most constant and characteristic ideas.

Second, Durkheim regarded it as very doubtful that the advance of civilization increases human happiness in any case. Here Durkheim initially sounds like Rousseau: while he admitted that we enjoy pleasures unknown to earlier societies, he observed also that we experience forms of suffering that they were spared, and added that it is not at all certain that the balance is in our favor. But it soon becomes clear that, again, Durkheim's more fundamental source was Aristotle. Even if social progress did produce more pleasure than pain, Durkheim thus insisted, this would not necessarily bring more happiness; for "pleasure" describes the local, limited, momentary

12. Durkheim also argued that even these limited pleasures follow their causes by considerable periods of time; thus, those generations inaugurating such advances experience not pleasure but pain, and thus the expectation of pleasure could hardly have been their motive.

state of a particular function, while "happiness" describes the health of the physical and moral species in its entirety, the extent to which that species has realized its true nature. Thus, the normal savage is just as happy as the normal civilized man, an argument supported not only by Waitz's *Anthropologie der Naturvölker* (1859), but also by the rapid rise in the suicide rate commensurate with the advance in civilization, a phenomenon in which Durkheim already had a powerful interest.

Durkheim's third argument dealt with a revised version of the "happiness hypothesis" which might have met the objections of his first two—that pleasure (which is at least an element in happiness) loses its intensity with repetition, and can be recaptured only through new stimuli, meaning more productive work (and hence, through the division of labor). Progress would thus be, quite literally, an effect of boredom. But to this Durkheim had several objections. First, such a "law" would apply to all societies, and thus it could provide no account of why the division of labor advances in some societies and not in others. Second, Durkheim denied the assumption on which the argument is based: namely, that repetition alone reduces the intensity of pleasure. So long as our pleasures have a certain variety, he argued, they can be repeated endlessly; only if the pleasure is continuous and uninterrupted does its intensity wane. But even if continuity thus does what repetition cannot, Durkheim continued, it could not inspire us with a need for new stimuli; for if continuity eliminates our consciousness of the agreeable state, we could hardly perceive that the pleasure attached to it has also vanished. Even novelty itself is but a secondary, accessory quality of pleasure, without which our ordinary pleasures, if sufficiently varied, can survive very well. In short, boredom is an insufficient cause to so painful and laborious an effect as the development of the division of labor.

Having thus dismissed individualistic, psychologistic causes, Durkheim argued that we must seek the explanation of the division of labor in some variation within the social context, and added that his earlier discussion of its function already pointed in the direction of an answer. Durkheim had shown how the organized structure (and thus the division of labor) had developed as the segmental structure had disappeared; thus, either the disappearance of the segmental structure is the cause of the division of labor, or vice versa. Since, as we have seen, the segmental structure is an insurmountable obstacle to the division of labor, the latter hypothesis is clearly false; the division of labor can thus appear only in proportion as the segmental structure has already begun to disappear.

How does this occur? Briefly, Durkheim suggested that, instead of social life being concentrated in a number of small, identical individual segments, these parts begin to extend beyond their limits, exchange movements, and act and react upon one another. Durkheim called this *dynamic* or *moral density*, and suggested that it increases in direct ratio to the progress of the division of labor. But what produces this "moral density"? Durkheim pointed to two causes. First, the real, material distance between members of a society must be reduced both spatially (e.g., the growth of cities) and technologically (e.g., advances in communications and transportation), for such "material density" multiplies the number of intra-societal relations. Second, this effect is reinforced by the sheer "social volume" of a society (the total number of its members). Thus, Durkheim argued that the division of labor varies in direct ratio to the dynamic or moral density of society, which is itself an effect of both material density and social volume.[13]

But how does this double cause (material density and social volume) produce its ultimate effect (the division of labor)? Here again, Durkheim had to confront the competing explanation of Herbert Spencer. In *First Principles* (1862), Spencer had argued that all homogeneous masses are inherently unstable and thus tend toward differentiation, and that they differentiate more rapidly and completely as their extension is greater. But in Spencer's theory, such extension produces differentiation, not by itself, but only in so far as it exposes parts of the social mass to diverse physical environments, thus encouraging diverse aptitudes and institutional specialization. Durkheim in fact agreed that a diversity of external circumstances has this differentiating effect; but he denied that this diversity was sufficient to *cause* (rather than merely *accelerate*) an effect so dramatic as the division of labor.

For his own explanation, Durkheim turned to Darwin's *Origin of Species* (1859), arguing that an increased material density and social volume cause the division of labor, not because they increase exposure to diverse external circumstances, but because they render the struggle for existence more acute. According to Darwin, so long as resources are plentiful and population size is limited, similar

13. Durkheim acknowledged that Comte had already come to much the same conclusion, citing *Cours de philosophie positive*, IV, 455.

organisms can live side by side in relative peace; but where population increases and resources become scarce, conflict and competition ensue, and this conflict is just as active as the organisms are similar and pursue similar needs. Where organisms are different and pursue different needs, on the other hand, what is useful to one organism will be of no value to another, and conflict will diminish.

Human populations, Durkheim argued, adhere to the same law. In so far as a social structure is "segmental" in character, each segment has its own organs, kept apart from like organs by the divisions between segments. With the growth in the "material density" and "social volume" of the society, these divisions disappear, the similar organs are put into contact with one another, and competition between them ensues. Those groups which triumph then have a larger task, which can be discharged only through a greater internal division of labor; those organs which are vanquished can henceforth maintain themselves only by specializing on a fraction of the social function they previously performed; but in either case, the division of labor is advanced.

Thus, the conflict and competition resulting from an increase in social volume and density produces advances in the division of labor, just as the latter mitigates against the negative consequences of the former. In the modern city, for example, large and highly condensed populations can coexist peacefully as a consequence of occupational differentiation: "The soldier seeks military glory, the priest moral authority, the statesman power, the businessman riches, the scholar scientific renown. Each of them can attain his end without preventing the others from obtaining theirs" (1893: 267). Nothing in this process, Durkheim added, implies an increase in happiness, or that the pursuit of happiness might be its goal: on the contrary, "everything takes place mechanically" as the result of an inexorable law of social progress.

Finally, Durkheim argued, it is a corollary of this law that the division of labor can be established only among the members of an already constituted society. For the effect of these same forces (e.g., opposition, conflict, competition, etc.) upon a number of independent individuals could only be further diversification without the development of compensatory social bonds,[14] while Durkheim had already shown that the division of labor creates moral linkages even

14. Here Durkheim cited the support of Darwin's "law of the divergence of characters" (cf. 1893: 276).

as it differentiates. Durkheim thus argued that the individuals among whom the struggle for existence is waged must already belong to the same, mechanically solidary society. In opposition to Spencer's view that a society is the product of cooperation, therefore, Durkheim supported Comte's argument that cooperation already presupposes the spontaneous existence of society.[15] This, in turn, became the basis for Durkheim's reply to Brunètiere at the height of the Dreyfus Affair. Far from being destructive of the social order, individualism is itself the product of society, and expresses a particular stage in its ongoing, structural evolution.

Durkheim had thus argued forcefully that the division of labor is caused by changes in the volume and density of societies. But this was not yet a complete explanation, for Durkheim recognized that such specialization was not the only possible solution to the struggle for existence which then ensued. Others included emigration, colonization, resignation to a precarious existence, and even suicide. The division of labor was thus a contingent rather than a necessary consequence of changes in the social environment, and for it rather than its alternatives to result, it was essential that the influence of at least two secondary factors—the *conscience collective* and heredity—be significantly reduced.

Durkheim's argument concerning the "progressive indetermination" of the *conscience collective* has already been described; but now Durkheim attempted to explain it, focusing equally on the growth of rationality and the decline of tradition. In early societies, Durkheim began, everyone is related to specific objects of their environment (e.g., animals, trees, plants, etc.) in roughly the same way, and the states of *conscience* representing this environment take on a parallel similarity; the fusion of these individual *consciences* thus results in a *conscience collective* which is sharp, decisive, and well-defined. As these societies become more voluminous and their populations more diversely situated, however, common objects can no longer create common experiences and representations; in so far as it is to remain "common," therefore, the *conscience collective* must necessarily become less concrete and well-defined, and more general and abstract. The "animal" becomes the "species," the "tree" becomes "trees in general and *in abstracto*," the "Greek" and the "Roman" become the concept of "man"; and a similar process of progressive

---

15. Durkheim's citations are to Spencer, *Principles of Sociology*, III, 331; and Comte, *Cours de philosophie positive*, IV, 421.

abstraction up to the level of universalizable concepts persists in law, religion, and morality. This explains the difficulty we have in understanding primitive societies. Our own minds, dominated by the logic and rationality this evolutionary process has produced, see in earlier societies only bizarre, fortuitous combinations of hetero-geneous elements; but in fact, these are simply societies dominated by concrete sensations and representations rather than abstract concepts.[16]

But in so far as the *conscience collective* thus becomes less concrete and decisive, it necessarily has less of an impact on individual thought and behavior. Precise states of *conscience* act in a manner analogous to instinctive reflexes; more general principles affect behavior only through the intervening reflections of intelligence. Thus, "deliber-ated movements have not the spontaneity of involuntary movements. Because it becomes more rational, the [*conscience collective*] becomes less imperative, and for this very reason, it wields less restraint over the free development of individuals" (1893: 290–291). But the cause of this growth of rationality, again, is the increase in the volume of the society's population and the environmental diversity thus implied.

Still more important than the "progressive indetermination" of the *conscience collective*, however, is the decline of tradition; for the strength of the *conscience* is due to the fact not only that its states are shared, but also that they are the legacy of previous generations. This authority of tradition is well supported in societies of the segmental type, which, as we have seen, have a familial as well as a political base; but as the segmental organization is undermined, individuals no longer feel bound to their kin-group or even their place of origin; migration ensues, and the authority of tradition weakens commensur-ately. But here, again, the decline of tradition is the consequence of those factors—social volume and density—which gradually dissipate the segmental form of social organization. In other words, just as it is purely mechanical causes which lead to the individual's submersion in the *conscience collective*, it is similarly mechanical causes (*not* the "utility" of emancipation) which subvert that *conscience* and lead to individual freedom.

But don't the occupational specialities of more organized societies simply reproduce the *conscience* of the primitive segment, and

16. This was the source of Durkheim's later, extended disagreement with Lucien Lévy-Bruhl (see Chapter 5 below).

exercise the same regulative function? For at least three reasons, Durkheim's answer was an emphatic *no*: first, the occupational *conscience* affects only the occupational life, beyond which the individual enjoys much greater freedom; second, the occupational *conscience* is shared by fewer individual minds, has commensurately less authority, and thus offers less resistance to individual transgressions than its collective counterpart; and third, the same causes (i.e., increased volume and density) which progressively undermine the *conscience collective* have a similar, if less dramatic, effect within the occupational group. Thus, "not only does occupational regulation, because of its very nature, hinder less than any other the play of individual variation, but it also tends to do so less and less" (1893: 303).

The other "secondary factor" whose influence had to be reduced in order for the division of labor to emerge was the role of heredity. Durkheim was particularly concerned with this because, according to John Stuart Mill's *Principles of Political Economy* (1848), the first condition of the division of labor was that "diversity of natures" whose principal function was to classify individuals according to their capacities. If this were the case, Durkheim argued, heredity would constitute an even more insurmountable obstacle to individual variability than the *conscience collective*; for, where the latter chained us only to the moral authority of our familial group, the former would bind us to our race, and thus to an utterly impersonal, congenital past, totally oblivious to our individual interests and aspirations. Thus, the greater the role of heredity in a society's distribution of tasks (as, for example, in the caste system, or in rigidly stratified societies), the more invariable that distribution, and the more difficult it is for the division of labor to make headway. It was Durkheim's goal, however, to show that, for at least two reasons, the role played by heredity in the distribution of tasks has declined in the course of social evolution.

First, Durkheim observed, aptitudes appear to be less transmissible by heredity precisely to the degree that they are more specialized; in so far as a society has a more complex division of labor, therefore, the relative role played by heredity in determining individual capacities will have been reduced. In short, social evolution produces new modes of activity requiring capacities that heredity simply cannot transmit. Second, Durkheim insisted, even those capacities that heredity *can* transmit (e.g., instincts) decline both in number and strength with social evolution.[17] Whether conceived relatively or absolutely, therefore, the contribution of heredity to the determination of individual tasks has been progressively reduced, and has thus presented few obstacles to the continuing growth of the division of labor.

This led Durkheim to some general conclusions about the distinction between the division of physiological labor and its social counterpart. Precisely because it is imposed by birth, Durkheim argued, the function of the biological cell is immutably fixed; but in society, hereditary dispositions are not predestinary, and the individual's specialized function is largely self-determined. Durkheim thus denied the view of Comte and Spencer that "substitution" (i.e., one part of an aggregate exchanging function with another) was a characteristic of lower rather than higher evolutionary forms;[18] on the contrary, in social evolution, function becomes independent of structure in direct proportion to the increasing complexity of society. This in turn explains the origin and development of "civilization"; for, as social volume and density increase, men can maintain themselves only through harder work and the intensification of their faculties, which inevitably produces a higher state of culture.

But Durkheim's theory of social evolution was not quite so mechanistic as the account above implies; for, while he urged that civilization was thus the effect of necessary causes, and denied that it was the result of the desire for happiness, he nonetheless argued that it was also "an end, an object of desire, in short, an ideal" (1893: 339). This paradoxical quality of civilization was based, once again, on Durkheim's distinction between the normal and the pathological. At each stage in the history of a given society, he suggested, there is a "certain intensity" of the collective life which is "normal"; and if everything in the society happens "normally," this state is realized automatically. But, in fact, everything does *not* happen normally; societies, like individual organisms, are subject to disease, and this prevents them from realizing their natural, ideal condition. Under these circumstances, Durkheim argued, it is not only legitimate but

17. Durkheim corroborated this argument with the observation that even that degree of physiological conformity required to speak meaningfully of a "race" at all seems rapidly to be disappearing, and added an extended commentary on Sir Francis Galton's *Natural Inheritance* (1889) both to confirm and explain it (cf. 1893: 323–327).

18. Durkheim here cites Comte, *Cours de philosophie positive*, VI, 505; and Spencer, *Principles of Sociology*, II, 57.

also essential that the sociologist intervene, ascertain the degree of collective activity appropriate to existing conditions, and attempt to realize this ideal state of health (or "golden mean") by the proper means.[19] And precisely because the "conditions" here referred to would constantly change, the social ideal would always be *definite* without ever becoming *definitive*: "Thus, not only does a mechanistic theory of progress not deprive us of an ideal, but it permits us to believe that we shall never lack for one" (1890: 344).[20]

Finally, these observations led Durkheim to a sociological re-formulation of the mind–body problem posed in Descartes' *Meditations* (1641). The progress of the individual *conscience*, as we have seen, is in inverse ratio to that of instinct, not because that *conscience* "breaks up" instinct, but because it "invades" the territory that instinct has ceased to occupy. Instinct, of course, has regressed because of the increasing importance of sociability; thus, the rational superiority of human beings over lower animals is a consequence of their superior sociability. Durkheim thus agreed with the observation of the "spiritualist" philosophers[21] that modern "psycho-physiology" would never be able to explain more than a small fraction of psychic phenomena through reference to organic causes; for psychic life, in its highest manifestations, is simply much too free and complex to be understood as a mere extension of physical life. But this is not to say that psychic life cannot be explained by natural causes; for society, no less than organic processes, is a part of nature. There is thus a vast region of the individual *conscience* which is both unintelligible to "psycho-physiology" and yet perfectly amenable to scientific investigation. Durkheim thus called for a "socio-psychology" which would investigate those psychic facts which have social causes. Far from deriving social facts from the essential features of human nature, such a positive science, *pace* Spencer, would derive human nature from society.

19. For Durkheim of course, these means included, above all else, moral education, and excluded, without qualification, revolutionary political activity (cf. 1893: 340–341).

20. This was Durkheim's answer to Spencer's argument, presented first in *Social Statics* (1850) and extended in *First Principles* (1862), that social evolution has a limit, beyond which it cannot pass, in the perfect adaptation of the individual to the natural environment.

21. In French philosophy, the term "spiritualism" is typically reserved for Maine de Biran (1766–1824), Felix Ravaisson-Mollien (1813–1900), and Henri Bergson (1859–1941).

ABNORMAL FORMS OF THE DIVISION OF LABOR

The normal function of the division of labor, as we have seen, is to produce a form of social solidarity; but, like all social (as well as biological) facts, the division of labor may present "pathological" forms which produce different and even contrary results. Durkheim was especially concerned to study these forms for two reasons: first, if it could not be proved that they were deviant and exceptional, the division of labor might be accused of "logically implying" them; and second, the study of such deviant forms might help us better to understand those conditions supportive of the normal state. Eventually Durkheim focused on three types of such pathological forms, not because they exhausted the range of deviant cases, but because they seemed the most general and most serious.

The first type, already identified by Comte,[22] is found where individuals, increasingly isolated by their more specialized tasks, lose any sense of being integral parts of some larger whole. This reflects a lack of mutual adjustment among the parts of the social organism which Durkheim called the *anomic division of labor*, citing certain commercial and industrial crises, the conflict between capital and labor, and the "scholastic" specialization of scientific investigation among its examples. And what was particularly alarming, again, was that this form of social disintegration increased with the growth of the division of labor, and thus appeared to be its natural rather than pathological consequence.

How was such a consequence to be avoided? Comte's answer, based on his acceptance of the view that social integration is not a spontaneous product of the division of labor, was that an independent, governmental organ (i.e., the state, as informed by the positive philosophy) was necessary to realize and maintain social unity. Durkheim, by contrast, was extremely skeptical of the efficacy of government regulation of the economy; for the problems afflicting economic institutions arose from a multiplicity of particular circumstances of which only those closest to those problems have any knowledge. And, in any case, he rejected Comte's premise as well; as with all organisms, the unity of society was to be obtained by the "spontaneous consensus of parts" (1893: 360).

To overcome the anomic division of labor, therefore, we must first

22. Durkheim cites *Cours de philosophie positive*, IV, 429; and Espinas, *Les Sociétés animaux* (1877).

determine the conditions essential to the normal state of organic solidarity. These conditions include not only a system of organs necessary to one another, but also the predetermination of the *way* in which these mutually necessary organs and their functions are to be related. This predetermination is the critical role of rules of conduct, which are themselves the product of habit and tradition. Very briefly, certain groups of people (organs) engage in definite forms of action (functions) which are repeated because they cling to the constant conditions of social life; when the division of labor brings these different organs and their functions together, the relations thus formed partake of the same degree of fixity and regularity; and these relations, being repeated, become habitual, and, when collective force is added, are transformed into rules of conduct.

The difficulty with the anomic division of labor, of course, is that such rules either do not exist or are not in accord with the degree of development of the division of labor. How can such a situation arise? Typically, something is interposed between otherwise contiguous organs so that the mutual stimulation created by their functions becomes less frequent, less intense, and less determined; the organs lose the sense of mutual dependence that mutual stimulation would normally create, and, as a consequence, the rules reflecting those relations remain vague, ill-defined, and fail to perform their proper integrative function. In commercial and industrial crises, for example, the growth and separation of producers and their markets has proceeded to the extent that the former cannot rationally predict the behavior of the latter; in the conflict between labor and capital, the development of large-scale industry and the factory system has separated the worker both from his family and from his employer; and in the specialization of scientific investigation, the moral and social sciences in particular have not yet understood their relationship to one another and to the older sciences, and have thus ignored the collaborative nature of the work in which they are engaged. But in each case, anomie is the consequence not of the division of labor itself, but of those exceptional and abnormal circumstances under which otherwise contiguous organs become separated, thus preventing the adequate development of rules of conduct.

But it is not sufficient simply that there be rules, for sometimes the rules themselves are the source of the problems. Where the lower classes become dissatisfied with the position granted them by custom or law, for example, we find a strictly regulated form of organization which Durkheim called the *forced division of labor*, which is nonetheless a potential source of dissension and civil war. The causes of this pathological form are clear. In society, as we have seen, there is a great distance between the hereditary dispositions of the individual and the social function he will fill; and the "space" thus left open to striving and deliberation is also vulnerable to influences which deflect the individual from the role most consistent with his tastes, aptitudes, and capacities. But for the division of labor to produce solidarity, it is not sufficient that each individual have his specialized task; it is still necessary that this task be appropriate to him. The "forced division of labor" is thus the consequence of that structural condition in which the distribution of social functions does not correspond to the distribution of natural talents.

Again, Durkheim insisted that this condition was not a necessary consequence of the division of labor, but rather the product of particular circumstances. "Normally" the division of labor arises spontaneously, and the harmony between individual natures and social functions is the inevitable consequence of each individual's unimpeded pursuit of those tasks for which he is best suited. But here the difficulty arises. For *social* inequalities thus to express no more than *natural* inequalities requires a social context in which the latter can be neither increased nor decreased by any external cause; in other words, it requires absolute equality of external conditions, and Durkheim was well aware that no such society had ever existed.

Durkheim was thus in the seemingly awkward position of defining as "normal" a feature which the division of labor had never presented in its pure state. Nonetheless, as always, he was optimistic. Pointing to the progressive decline of the caste system, the increasing accessibility of public office to the average citizen, and the growth of social assistance whereby the disadvantages of birth could be overcome, Durkheim argued not simply that progress toward social justice had been made or that it was a good to be pursued, but that the elimination of external inequalities and realization of the ideal of structural spontaneity was essential—indeed, indispensable—to that form of solidarity upon which "organized" societies themselves depend. Social justice would emerge, quite literally, because it *had to* if advanced societies were to exist at all.

Equality of external conditions was thus necessary if each individual was to find his proper function in society; but it was also necessary if these functions were to be linked to one another. This was particularly evident in contractual relations, which are the juridical expression of those exchanges necessary to the division of labor. Precisely because such exchanges between functions in advanced societies are necessary, contracts must be kept; but unless contractual relations were to remain precarious, they must be kept not just through fear of force, but spontaneously. And it is to fulfill this condition of spontaneity that we say contracts must involve "free consent."

But what does "free consent" mean? In order to answer this question, Durkheim first had to define his notion of the "social value" of an object of exchange. Such a value, Durkheim insisted, is equivalent not (*pace* Ricardo) to the labor the object might have cost, but to the amount of energy capable of producing "useful social effects" which the object contains; this, in turn, varies according to the sum of efforts necessary to produce the object, the intensity of the needs which it satisfies, and the extent of the satisfaction it brings. The *price* of an object deviates from this value, Durkheim argued, only under "abnormal" conditions; thus, the public finds "unjust" every exchange where the price of the object bears no relation to the trouble it cost and the social service it renders. According to Durkheim, therefore, a contract is "freely consented to" only if the services exchanged have an equivalent social value, expressing an equilibrium of wills which is consecrated by a contract; and because this equilibrium is produced and maintained by itself, and expresses the nature of things, it is truly spontaneous.

For the obligatory force of a contract to be complete, therefore, expressed consent alone is not sufficient; the contract must also be just. Social value, however, cannot be determined *a priori*, but only in the process of exchange itself; thus, for justice to be the rule of contracts, it is necessary, once again, for the contracting parties (labor and management) to be placed in conditions that are externally equal. And here again, Durkheim revealed his evolutionary optimism: the emphasis on "consent" (and especially "free" consent) appears as a very recent development, and contractual law increasingly detracts value from those contracts entered under unequal conditions. If a strong *conscience collective* was the pre-emptive need of all lower societies, the requirement and ideal goal of modern societies is social justice.

Durkheim's third pathological form of the division of labor arose from his observation that the functions of an organism can become more active only on the condition that they also become more continuous—one organ can do more only if the other organs do more, and vice versa. Where this continuity is lacking, the functional activity of the specialized parts decreases, resulting in wasted effort and loss of productive capacity; but, as always, Durkheim was less concerned with the economic than with the moral consequences of such an abnormal condition. Where the functional activity of the parts languishes, Durkheim thus warned, the solidarity of the whole is undermined.

For precisely this reason, the first concern of intelligent, scientific management will be to suppress useless tasks, to distribute work so that each worker is sufficiently occupied, and thus to maximize the functional activity of each social organ. Increased activity in turn produces greater continuity, an augmented sense of the mutual dependence of the parts on one another, and a stronger bond of solidarity. But where mismanagement prevails, the activity of each worker is reduced, functions become discontinuous, and solidarity is undermined.

But again, Durkheim insisted that such mismanagement and inactivity is the exception rather than the rule, a judgment for which he gave at least four reasons. First, the same factors that cause us to specialize (the increase in social volume and density) also cause us to work harder, for the competition *within* each speciality increases as the specialities themselves become more numerous and divided. Second, the division of labor itself, by saving time otherwise wasted in passing from one function to another, increases the efficiency of the individual worker. Third, functional activity grows with the talent and competence of the individual worker, and both are naturally increased by the repetition of similar tasks. And finally, as labor becomes divided, work becomes a permanent occupation, then a habit, and ultimately a need—a progression which increases the functional activity of all workers subject to it.

What, then, is the "first principle" of ethics? And what is the relation of ethics to society? Among the most incontestable of moral rules, Durkheim observed, is that which orders us to internalize the *conscience collective* of the groups to which we belong; and the "moral" quality of this rule is derived from the essential function it serves in preventing social disintegration. But the contrary rule, which orders us to specialize, is no less imperative; and it too is "moral" because obedience to it, after a certain stage in social evolution, is essential to social cohesion. An initial answer to both questions above, therefore, is that moral rules render "society" possible: "Everything which is a source of solidarity is moral, everything which forces man to take account of other men is moral, everything which forces him to regulate his conduct through something other than the striving of his ego is moral, and morality is as solid as these ties are numerous and strong" (1893: 398).

Durkheim thus opposed the more Kantian tradition which removed moral consciousness from its societal context and defined it through freedom of the will. On the contrary, morality consists in a state of social dependence, and thus deprives the individual of some freedom of movement; and society, far from consisting of external threats to the autonomy of the will, provides the sole foundation upon which that will can act: "Let all social life disappear," Durkheim argued, "and moral life will disappear with it, since it would no longer have any objective" (1893: 399). Even Kant's "duties of the individual towards himself" are properly understood as duties toward society, for they are the product of collective sentiments which the individual must not offend. The "categorical imperative" of modern society, therefore, is to concentrate and specialize our activities, contract our horizons, choose a definite task, and immerse ourselves in it completely.

The predictable objection to this injunction, of course, was that such specialization implies a narrowing of the individual personality, rendering each of us an "incomplete" human being. But why, Durkheim asked, is it more natural to develop superficially rather than profoundly? Why is there more dignity in being "complete" and mediocre rather than in living a more specialized, but intense, existence? Durkheim, in other words, was re-invoking the Aristotelian principle that man ought to realize his nature *as man*, though with the added caveat that this nature is not historically constant, but rather varies according to the needs of the societal type in question. Moreover, to be a "person" means to be an *autonomous source of action*, to possess something empirical and concrete which is ours and ours alone; and this condition, by sharp contrast with the "apparent" liberty and "borrowed" personality of individuals in lower societies, is the product of the division of labor.

While Durkheim thus shared the sense of some contemporaries that theirs was an age of profound crisis, he denied that the crisis was intellectual or "spiritual" in its causes. On the contrary, it was the consequence of far-reaching structural changes undergone by society in a very short time; thus, while the morality corresponding to the segmental societal type had regressed, the "new" morality of the organized type had not advanced rapidly enough to fill the void thereby left in our *consciences*. The corrective for this crisis, therefore, was not to resuscitate the outworn dogmas of the past, but to reduce external inequality and increase justice, and thus to render the new, still discordant organs and functions harmonious. This was an enterprise, Durkheim concluded, in which social structure set the terms, while social theory set the goals:

> In short, our first duty is to make a moral code for ourselves. Such a work cannot be improvised in the silence of the study; it can arise only through itself, little by little, under the pressure of internal causes which make it necessary. But the service that thought can and must render is in fixing the goal that we must attain. (1893: 409)

CRITICAL REMARKS

The Division of Labor in Society was a seminal contribution to the sociology of law and morality, and remains a sociological "classic" by any standards. By the same standards, however, it also contains undeniable shortcomings which have limited its appeal to modern sociologists. An immediate difficulty, for example, is Durkheim's insistence that social solidarity is an exclusively "moral" phenomenon, of which law is the "externally visible symbol," an insistence which ignores the frequent conflict of some moral principles with others, some laws with other laws, and morality with legality generally. Durkheim, of course, did not deny the existence of such conflict; but he did suggest that it was "pathological," not a part of the "normal" functioning of society, and thus placed it beyond the central focus of his sociological vision. Similarly, Durkheim implied that the state is merely an instrument whose authority reflects the disposition of the *conscience collective*, an implication which excludes most of the concerns explored so brilliantly by Max Weber—the means by which one group in a society achieves asymmetrical control over another; the personal, subjective standards by which the first judges the behavior of the second and renders it consequential; and so on. The point here is not simply that Durkheim did not choose to discuss these issues; rather, the point is that he *could* not, given the reasons why he chose to study law in the first place—as an "external index" of the more fundamental moral conditions of the social order (cf. Lukes and Scull, 1983: 5–8).

Second, Durkheim clearly overstated the role of repressive law relative to the institutions of interdependence and reciprocity (e.g., kinship, religious ritual, economic and political alliance, etc.) in primitive societies. Malinowski's *Argonauts of the Western Pacific* (1922), for example, has provided ample evidence of the significance and complexity of relations of exchange among the Trobriand Islanders. In part, this may be attributed to Durkheim's ignorance (or rather dismissal) of the ethnographic literature on primitive peoples, for his pronouncements on "primitive" legal systems in *The Division of Labor* are largely based on inferences drawn from the Hebrew Torah, the Twelve Tables of the ancient Romans, and the laws of early Christian Europe; but he seems to have got these wrong as well. The religious and moral exhortations of the Torah, for example, are largely devoid of "penal" sanctions, and coexisted with a predominantly secular legal system maintained by their "restitutive" counterparts; the sanctions attached to the Twelve Tables were almost equally restitutive; and the gradual emergence of the state as the pre-emptive legal institution of early modern Europe witnessed an *increase* in the relative proportion of repressive laws. Indeed, Durkheim understated the role of repressive law even in advanced industrial societies, in part because he ignored the fact that the nineteenth-century system of penal incarceration replaced the custom of compensating the victims of some crimes financially, and in part because he disregarded the punitive, stigmatizing aspect of many civil laws (cf. Lukes and Scull, 1983: 10–15).

Finally, it is difficult to share Durkheim's confidence in the self-regulating quality of organic solidarity. Durkheim's account of the "anomic" division of labor alone, for example, exposed all the evils of unregulated capitalism—commercial and industrial crises, class conflict, meaningless, alienated labor, etc. (Lukes, 1972: 174). But his analysis of these evils was notoriously uncritical; because organic solidarity has evolved more slowly than its mechanical counterpart has passed away, the Third Republic endures a "pathological, disintegrative void"—an analysis which simultaneously implies that these evils are not endemic to modern societies (and thus eviscerates any criticism of them), and conveniently locates the conditions for the successful functioning of "organized" societies in some unspecified, Utopian future. As his work developed, however, Durkheim gradually relinquished the evolutionary optimism which underlay this "mechanical, self-regulating" conception of the division of labor, became increasingly attracted to socialism and the potentially regulatory function of occupational groups,[23] and granted greater emphasis to the independent role of collective beliefs in social life.

23. Cf. the preface to the second edition of *The Division of Labor in Society* (1902a).

3

Studying Social Facts:
The Rules of Sociological Method (1895)

WHAT IS A SOCIAL FACT?

The reader of *The Division of Labor in Society* would have understood that "sociology" is a science which, like biology, studies the phenomena of the natural world and, like psychology, studies human actions, thoughts, and feelings. What he might not have understood was that Durkheim conceived of sociology as the scientific study of a reality *sui generis*, a clearly defined group of phenomena different from those studied by all other sciences, biology and psychology included. It was for these phenomena that Durkheim reserved the term *social facts*, i.e., "a category of facts which present very special characteristics: they consist of manners of acting, thinking, and feeling external to the individual, which are invested with a coercive power by virtue of which they exercise control over him" (1895: 52). Since these facts consisted of actions, thoughts, and feelings, they could not be confused with biological phenomena; but neither were they the province of psychology, for they existed outside the individual *conscience*. It was to define the proper method for their study that Durkheim wrote *The Rules of Sociological Method* (1895).

Durkheim was particularly concerned to distinguish social facts, which he sometimes described as "states of the collective mind," from the forms these states assumed when manifested through private, individual minds. This distinction is most obvious in cases like those treated in *The Division of Labor*—e.g., customs, moral and legal rules, religious beliefs, etc.—which indeed appear to have an existence independent of the various actions they determine. It is considerably less obvious, however, where the social fact in question is among those more elusive "currents of opinion" reflected in lower or higher birth, migration, or suicide rates; and for the isolation of these from their individual manifestations, Durkheim recommended the use of statistics, which "cancel out" the influence of individual conditions by subsuming all individual cases in the statistical aggregate.[1] Durkheim did not deny, of course, that such individual manifestations were in some sense "social," for they were indeed manifestations of states of the collective mind; but precisely because they also depended in part on the psychological and biological constitution of the individual, as well as his particular circumstances, Durkheim reserved for them the term "socio-psychical," suggesting that they might remain of interest to the sociologist without constituting the immediate subject matter of sociology (cf. 1893: 345–350).[2]

It might still be argued, of course, that the external, coercive power of social facts is *derived from* their being held in common by most of the individual members of a society; and that, in this sense, the characteristics of the whole are the product of the characteristics of the parts. But there was no proposition to which Durkheim was more opposed. The obligatory, coercive nature of social facts, he argued, is repeatedly manifested in individuals because it is imposed upon them, particularly through education; the parts are thus derived from the whole rather than the whole from the parts.[3]

But how is the presence of a social fact to be recognized? Durkheim gave two answers, one pointing backward to *The Division of Labor*, the other forward to *Suicide*. Because the essential trait of social facts is their external coercive power, Durkheim first suggested that they could be recognized by the existence of some predetermined legal sanction or, in the case of moral and religious beliefs, by their reaction to those forms of individual belief and action which

1. The classic demonstration of this point, of course, was Durkheim's *Suicide* (1897); cf. Chapter 4 below.

2. Durkheim saw such facts as analogous to those "mixed" phenomena of nature studied by "combined" sciences such as biochemistry.

3. This, of course, had been a major source of Durkheim's disagreement with Spencer in *The Division of Labor* (cf. 1893: 200–229). In *Rules*, Durkheim extended the same argument to oppose the "ingenious system" of Gabriel Tarde: "imitation," like "generality," is viewed as the consequence rather than the cause of the coercive nature of a social fact (cf. 1895: 57).

they perceived as threatening. But where the exercise of social constraint is less direct, as in those forms of economic organization which give rise to anomie, their presence is more easily ascertained by their "generality combined with objectivity"—i.e., by how widespread they are within the group, while also existing independently of any particular forms they might assume. But whether direct or indirect, the essential defining characteristic of social facts remains their external, coercive power, as manifested through the constraint they exercise on the individual.

Finally, again invoking a distinction introduced in *The Division of Labor*, Durkheim insisted that social facts were not simply limited to ways of *functioning* (e.g., acting, thinking, feeling, etc.), but also extended to ways of *being* (e.g., the number, nature, and relation of the parts of a society, the size and geographical distribution of its population, the nature and extent of its communication networks, etc.).[4] The second class of "structural" facts, Durkheim argued, exhibits precisely the same characteristics of externality and coercion as the first—a political organization restricts our behavior no less than a political ideology, and a communication network no less than the thought to be conveyed. In fact, Durkheim insisted that there were not two "classes" at all, for the structural features of a society were nothing more than social functions which had been "consolidated" over long periods of time. Durkheim's "social fact" thus proved to be a conveniently elastic concept, covering the range from the most clearly delineated features of social structure (e.g., population size and distribution) to the most spontaneous currents of public opinion and enthusiasm.

RULES FOR THE OBSERVATION OF SOCIAL FACTS

In his *Novum Organum* (1620), Francis Bacon discerned a general tendency of the human mind which, together with the serious defects of the current learning, had to be corrected if his plan for the advancement of scientific knowledge was to succeed. This was the

---

4. The distinction corresponds to, and was to a considerable extent the source of, the more common sociological distinction between "structure" and "function," and for convenience these terms will be adopted henceforth. Pursuing the biological analogue, Durkheim also frequently employed the term "physiological" to refer to social function, and "anatomical" or "morphological" to refer to social structure.

quite natural tendency to take our *ideas* of things (what Bacon called *notiones vulgares, praenotiones*, or "idols") for the *things themselves*, and then to construct our "knowledge" of the latter on the foundation of the largely undisciplined manipulation of the former; and it was to overcome such false notions, and thus to restore man's lost mastery over the natural world, that Bacon had planned (but never completed) the Great Instauration.

It was appropriate that Durkheim should refer to Bacon's work in the *Rules*, for he clearly conceived of his own project in similar terms. Just as crudely formed concepts of natural phenomena necessarily precede scientific reflection upon them, and just as alchemy thus precedes chemistry and astrology precedes astronomy, so men have not awaited the advent of social science before framing ideas of law, morality, the family, the state, or society itself. Indeed, the seductive character of our *praenotiones* of society is even greater than were those of chemical or astronomical phenomena, for the simple reason that society is the product of human activity, and thus appears to be the expression of and even equivalent to the ideas we have of it. Comte's *Cours de philosophie positive* (1830–1842), for example, focused on the *idea* of the progress of humanity, while Spencer's *Principles of Sociology* (1876–1885) dismissed Comte's idea only to install his own preconception of "cooperation."

But isn't it possible that social phenomena really are the development and realization of certain ideas? Even were this the case, Durkheim responded, we do not know *a priori* what these ideas are, for social phenomena are presented to us only "from the outside"; thus, even if social facts ultimately do not have the essential features of things, we must begin our investigations as if they did. But, truer to form, Durkheim immediately reasserted his conviction of what Peter Berger has aptly called the *choséité* (literally, "thingness") of social facts. A "thing" is recognizable as such chiefly because it is intractable to all modification by mere acts of will; and it is precisely this property of resistance to the action of individual wills which characterizes social facts. The most basic rule of all sociological method, Durkheim thus concluded, is *to treat social facts as things*.

From this initial injunction, three additional rules for the observation of social facts necessarily follow. The first, implied in much of the discussion above, is that *one must systematically discard all preconceptions*. Durkheim thus added the method of Cartesian doubt to Bacon's caveats concerning *praenotiones*, arguing that the sociologist must deny himself the use of those concepts formed outside of science and for extra-scientific needs: "He must free himself from those fallacious notions which hold sway over the mind of the ordinary person, shaking off, once and for all, the yoke of those empirical categories that long habit often makes tyrannical" (1895: 73).

Second, *the subject matter of research must only include a group of phenomena defined beforehand by certain common external characteristics, and all phenomena which correspond to this definition must be so included.* Every scientific investigation, Durkheim insisted, must begin by defining that specific group of phenomena with which it is concerned; and if this definition is to be objective, it must refer not to some ideal conception of these phenomena, but to those properties which are both inherent in the phenomena themselves and externally visible at the earliest stages of the investigation. Indeed, this had been Durkheim's procedure in *The Division of Labor*, where he defined as "crimes" all those acts provoking the externally ascertainable reaction known as "punishment."

The predictable objection to such a rule was that it attributes to visible but superficial phenomena an unwarranted significance. When crime is defined by punishment, for example, is it not then *derived from* punishment? Durkheim's answer was no, for two reasons. First, the function of the definition is neither to explain the phenomenon in question nor to express its essence; rather, it is to establish contact with *things*, which can only be done through externalities. It is not punishment that causes crime, but it is through punishment that crime is revealed to us, and thus punishment must be the starting point of our investigation. Second, the constant conjunction of crime and punishment suggests that there is an indissoluble link between the latter and the essential nature of the former, so that, however "superficial," punishment is a good place to start the investigation (1895: 80–81).

Finally, *when the sociologist undertakes to investigate any order of social facts, he must strive to consider them from a viewpoint where they present themselves in isolation from their individual manifestations.* Science, as we have seen, must dismiss those *praenotiones* formed through common, extra-scientific experience, and create its concepts anew on the basis of systematically observable data. But Durkheim was also aware that, even in the natural sciences, sense experience itself could be subjective, so that observable data too "personal" to the observer were discarded, and only those exhibiting a required degree of objectivity were retained. Sociological observations ought to be equally objective, and thus social facts should be detached as completely as possible from the individual facts by which they are manifested. In particular, Durkheim thus endorsed the study of those aspects of social reality which had "crystallized"—legal and moral rules, the facts of social structure, proverbs and aphorisms, etc.—which were "fixed objects" and thus more impervious to subjective impressions and personal applications.

RULES FOR DISTINGUISHING THE NORMAL FROM THE PATHOLOGICAL

As indicated in Book Three of *The Division of Labor*, however, Durkheim felt that social facts exhibit both normal and pathological forms; and he now added that it was an important part of sociological method to provide rules for distinguishing between them. The primary objection to such a provision, of course, was that such judgments of value have no place in science, whose sole purpose is to tell us how causes produce their effects, but not what ends we ought to pursue. The practical utility of social science would thus be limited to revealing which causes produce which effects, thus offering us the means to produce causes at will. The ends resulting from these causes might then be pursued and achieved for reasons beyond those of science itself. Durkheim's response was that there are always several means to the achievement of any end, and that the determination of the former is thus no less an act of will than that of the latter.[5] Science, in short, must guide us in the determination of our highest goals. The problem is to find an objective criterion, externally ascertainable yet inherent in social facts themselves, which will allow us to distinguish scientifically between social health and social illness.

This was a problem not easily solved, and it was only after a tedious search that Durkheim's criterion was discovered in the ordinary distinction between that which is general and that which is exceptional. Social facts which are "normal," by this criterion, would simply be those found in most, if not all, individuals, within narrow

5. It was recognition of this need for reflective thought as a guide to action, Durkheim felt, which had so long preserved the "ideological method" disparaged earlier; but Durkheim insisted that the problem could be solved without sacrificing the claims of reason to those of ideology (cf. 1895: 86).

limits of variation. Social facts which are "pathological," by contrast, would be those encountered only in a minority of cases, and only for brief periods in the lifetime of the individual even where they occur (1895: 91).[6] If we adopt the term *average type* to refer to that purely hypothetical entity containing the most frequently occurring characteristics of the species in their most frequently occurring forms, therefore, a social fact would be "normal" in so far as it approximates that type, and "pathological" in so far as it deviates therefrom. And from this criterion, it is clear that what is normal or pathological can be so only in relation to a given species and, if that species varies over time, in relation to a specific stage in its development (1895: 92).[7] Hence Durkheim's first rule for the distinction of the normal from the pathological: *A social fact is normal for a given social type, viewed at a given phase of its development, when it occurs in the average society of that species, considered at the corresponding phase of its evolution.*

But if "generality" is thus the criterion by which we recognize the normality of a social fact, this criterion itself still requires an explanation. Durkheim's initial request for such an explanation was accompanied by two rather pragmatic observations: first, that the normality of the phenomenon would be less doubtful if it could be shown that its external sign (generality) was not merely "apparent," but "grounded in the nature of things"; and, second, that the practical application of the knowledge thus acquired would be facilitated by knowing not simply *what* we want, but *why* we want it. But Durkheim's more fundamental motivation was derived from his recognition that, in certain "transition periods" (such as that through which he was manifestly living), a fact of extraordinary generality can persist, through force of blind habit, despite its lack of any correspondence with the new conditions of existence. Having established by observation that a fact is general, therefore, the sociologist must still reconstruct the conditions which determined this general fact and decide whether they still pertain or, on the contrary, have changed;[8] in the first case the fact is "normal," while in the

6. The last condition, of course, describes Durkheim's view of all three of those "pathological" forms discussed in Book Three of *The Division of Labor* (cf. 1893: 353–395).

7. Cf. the point raised in Chapter 2 above, i.e., that what is "normal" for the savage is not "normal" for civilized man.

8. Precisely because this method of verification presupposes the designation of a fact as normal by the criterion of generality, Durkheim insisted that it remained a secondary method which must not be substituted for the first (cf. 1895: 96).

second, its normality is "merely apparent."[9] Hence Durkheim's second rule: *The results of the preceding method can be verified by demonstrating that the general character of the phenomenon is related to the general conditions of collective life in the social type under consideration* (1895: 97).

It was Durkheim's illustration of these rules, however, which provoked the immediate interest of his contemporaries; for the example he selected was *crime*, whose "pathological" character, by almost any other criterion, appeared indisputable. Nonetheless, Durkheim observed, crime exists in all societies of all kinds, and, despite centuries of effort at its annihilation, has rather increased with the growth of civilization; thus, "there is no phenomenon which represents more incontrovertibly all the symptoms of normality, since it appears to be closely bound up with the conditions of all collective life" (1895: 98).[10] But for Durkheim to describe crime as normal did not mean resignation to a necessary evil; on the contrary, it meant that crime was *useful*, "a factor in public health, an integrative element in any healthy society" (1895: 98).

Consider first its necessity. In Book One of *The Division of Labor*, Durkheim had shown that "crime" consists of an action which offends strong, well-defined collective feelings. For such actions to cease, therefore, those feelings would have to be reinforced in each and every individual to the degree of strength required to counteract the opposite feelings. But if this occurred, Durkheim added, those weaker states of the *conscience collective*, whose milder reactions previously acknowledged mere breaches of convention, would also be reinforced, and what was unconventional would thereby become criminal; and the elevation of all collective sentiments to a strength sufficient to stifle all dissentient voices was simply incompatible with the enormous diversity of those environments which condition the commensurate variability of individual *consciences*. Since there cannot be a society in which individuals do not diverge to some extent from the *conscience collective*, it is equally necessary that some of these deviations assume a criminal character.

Durkheim's more scandalous argument, however, was that crime is also *useful*, in both a direct and an indirect sense. The argument for

9. This was the procedure used by Durkheim in *The Division of Labor* to demonstrate the "normality" of declining religious faith.

10. Crime may of course exhibit abnormal forms, as in an excessively high rate for a given societal type; but the existence of crime itself, in any society, is normal.

indirect utility appeared again in *The Division of Labor*, where Durkheim had shown that the gradual evolution of law and morality itself reflects more fundamental transformations in a society's collective sentiments. For such sentiments to change, however, they can be only moderately intense, while the only condition under which crime could cease (see above) must necessarily be one in which collective sentiments had attained an unprecedented intensity. For moral consciousness to evolve at all, therefore, individual creativity must be permitted. The criminal thus becomes the price we pay for the idealist. More directly, as in the case of Socrates, the criminal and the idealist are sometimes the same, and the crime proves to be the anticipation of that morality still to come.

RULES FOR THE CONSTITUTION OF SOCIAL TYPES

According to the second rule in the previous section, a social fact can be labeled "normal" or "pathological" only in relation to a given social "type" or "species." Durkheim's next step was thus to set out rules for the constitution or classification of such species. In particular, he sought a *via media* between the historians, for whom each society is unique and incomparable, and the philosophers, for whom different societies are only various expressions of the fundamental attributes of "human nature." In other words, Durkheim was after an intermediate entity which would acknowledge the unity required by scientific generalization as well as the diversity inherent in the facts.

As the means to this end, Durkheim again endorsed the method advocated in Bacon's *Novum Organum*—namely, to look for decisive or crucial facts which, regardless of their number, have scientific value or interest.[11] But which facts are most "decisive" or "crucial"? Clearly, those facts which *explain* other facts; and in this sense, Durkheim admitted, explanation and classification are interdependent, and neither can proceed very far in the absence of the other. But at least we know where to start: societies are made up of parts, and their character must thus depend on the nature, number, and relations of the parts thus combined. Durkheim thus set about

11. Durkheim rejected the alternative method of detailed monographic comparison as inconsistent with the main purpose of classification, which is to substitute a limited number of types for an indefinite multiplicity of individuals (cf. 1895: 110–111).

classifying social types according to the same principle which had guided that activity in *The Division of Labor*, and eventually codified it in a rule: *We shall begin by classifying societies according to the degree of organization they manifest, taking as a base the perfectly simple society or the single-segment society. Within these classes different varieties will be distinguished, according to whether a complete coalescence of the initial segments takes place.*[12]

RULES FOR THE EXPLANATION OF SOCIAL FACTS

The titles of the first two books of *The Division of Labor*, as well as most of the arguments within them, attest to Durkheim's aversion for any "teleological" confusion of the *function* of a social fact with its *cause*.[13] This aversion followed naturally from Durkheim's preemptive rule of sociological method; for once we recognize that social facts are real things, resistive forces prevailing over individual wills, it becomes clear that no human need or desire, however imperious, could be sufficient to such an effect. Indeed, like the vestigial organs of its biological counterpart, a social fact sometimes exists without serving any vital need or desire whatsoever, either because it has never done so, or because its utility has passed while it persists from force of habit.[14] Needs and desires may intervene to hasten or retard social development, but they cannot themselves create any social fact; and even their intervention is the effect of more fundamental social causes.[15] *Therefore when one undertakes to explain a social*

12. The term "coalescence" refers to the degree of concentration of the component segments, and "complete coalescence" is achieved where these segments no longer affect the administrative or political organization of the society (cf. 1895: 115).

13. Here, again, the primary objects of Durkheim's criticisms are Auguste Comte and Herbert Spencer (cf. 1895: 195).

14. Here Durkheim sometimes seems to argue with himself. While insisting on the need for functional as well as causal explanations of social facts, for example, he states that a social fact must generally be useful if it, and, indeed, the society of which it is a part, are to survive (cf. 1895: 124–125). The most charitable interpretation lays special emphasis on the words "vital" and "generally."

15. This argument, incidentally, reflects Durkheim's profoundly uniformitarian conception of social evolution. If historical development depended on ends desired and purposes pursued, he observed, social facts would be as infinitely diverse as human desires and purposes themselves; but the extraordinary regularity with which the same facts appear under the same circumstances suggest that less variable causes are at work.

phenomenon, the efficient cause which produces it and the function[16] *it fulfills must be investigated separately.*

But what was thus denounced as *teleological* was at least equally disparaged as *psychologistic*, for Durkheim regarded these as no more than different descriptions of the same methodological blunder. Indeed, if society is only a system of means set up to achieve certain ends, then these ends must surely be individual, for prior to society only individuals could exist. The origin and development of society would thus be the result of individual minds, and the laws of sociology no more than corollaries of those of psychology. The organization of the family would thus be the consequence of the conjugal and parental emotions; economic institutions, that of the desire for wealth; morality, that of self-interest informed by the principle of utility; and religion, that of those emotions provoked by fear of nature or awe at the charismatic personality, or even the religious "instinct" itself. At the risk of repetition, Durkheim regarded such "explanations" as inadequate to that which was to be explained—namely, a group of facts external to the individual which exercises a coercive power over him: "It is not from within himself that can come the external pressure which he undergoes; it is therefore not what is happening within himself which can explain it" (1895: 128).

Here Durkheim faced two common objections. The first was that, since the sole elements of which society is composed are individuals, then the explanation of social phenomena must lie in psychological facts. To this objection Durkheim's habitual response was to revert to the biological analogue—i.e., the constituent molecules of the living cell are crude matter, yet the association of such cells produces life. The whole, in other words, is something greater than the sum of its parts. Similarly, the association of individual human beings creates a social reality of a new kind, and it is in the facts of that association rather than the nature of associated elements that the explanation for this new reality is to be found. Between sociology and psychology, therefore, there exists the same break in continuity as is found

16. As in *The Division of Labor* (cf. p. 49), Durkheim used the term "function" (rather than "end," "aim," or "object") advisedly. Even where dealing with the "function" of a social fact separately from its cause, the question was solely one of determining the nature of any correspondence between the fact and the general needs of the social organism, regardless of whether this correspondence was intentional. "All such questions of intention," Durkheim observed, "are ... too subjective to be dealt with scientifically" (1895: 123).

between biology and the physical or chemical sciences: " . . . every time a social phenomenon is directly explained by a psychological phenomenon," Durkheim thus concluded, "we may rest assured that the explanation is false" (1895: 129).

Acknowledging that society, once formed, is the proximate cause of social phenomena, however, a second objection insisted that the original causes of the association itself were psychological in nature. But however far back in history we go, Durkheim answered, the fact of association appears to be the most obligatory of all, for it is the origin of all other obligations. We are born into a family, granted a nationality, and given an education, without our choosing any of them; and it is these associations which in turn determine those more "voluntary" obligations in which we subsequently acquiesce. All societies are born of other societies, Durkheim concluded, and "in the whole course of social evolution there has not been a single time when individuals have really had to consult together to decide whether they would enter into collective life together, and into one sort of collective life rather than another" (1895: 130).

Durkheim thus arrived at another rule: *The determining cause of a social fact must be sought among the antecedent social facts and not among the states of the individual consciousness.* But the arguments which lead to this rule, Durkheim then added, apply equally to the *function* of a social fact—while a social fact may have repercussions which serve the individual, this is not the immediate reason for its existence; on the contrary, its function consists in the production of *socially* useful effects. Durkheim thus complemented the rule above with a second: *The function of a social fact must always be sought in the relationship that it bears to some social end.*[17]

But in which among its innumerable antecedent conditions is the determining cause of a social fact to be found? If the distinctive condition for the emergence of social (as opposed to psychological) phenomena consists in the fact of association, Durkheim argued, then social phenomena must vary according to how the constituent elements in a society are associated. Durkheim called this the *inner*

17. Durkheim did not deny that psychology held some relevance for sociology; on the contrary, the association of psychological facts whereby social facts are produced is similar to the association of primary psychological elements (e.g., sensations, reflexes, instincts, etc.) whereby the individual consciousness is made up. Durkheim thus considered an education in psychology even more important than one in biology as a preparation for a sociologist; but still, collective life does not derive from individual life, and the latter cannot explain the former (cf. 1895: 134–135).

environment of a society, and thus proposed still another rule: *The primary origin of social processes of any importance must be sought in the constitution of the inner social environment.*[18] The arguments presented in support of this rule largely reproduce[19] the discussion of "social volume" and "dynamic density" found in Book Two of *The Division of Labor.*

But doesn't this "inner environment" itself depend on other social causes, either inherent within the society itself, or involving interaction with other societies? Durkheim admitted that there are no "first causes" in science, and that a fact is "primary" only in the sense that it is general enough to explain many others. But the "inner social environment," he insisted, is precisely such a fact. The more specialized environments of particular groups *within* a society also affect its functions; but these groups are themselves subject to the influence of the general internal association, and are commensurately less important. A similarly reduced significance was granted to the *external* environment of neighboring societies: first, because its influence can be felt only through the prior mediation of the internal environment; and second, because this would make present social facts dependent on past events. The second consequence was particularly objectionable, for Durkheim always insisted that the relationship between past and present states of any society was merely chronological, and could be rendered *causal* only at the exorbitant cost of postulating, as had Comte and Spencer, a metaphysical "inner tendency" in social evolution.[20]

Finally, it is only in relation to the inner social environment that the "utilitarian value" (function) of a social fact can be measured; for among the changes caused by that environment, only those are useful which correspond in some way with the most essential conditions of

18. The "constituent elements" of this environment are not limited to persons, but include both material and non-material objects (e.g., literature, art, law, custom, etc.) which also influence the direction and rapidity of social evolution. While these must be taken into consideration in an attempted explanation, however, Durkheim denied that they possessed the "motivating power" to produce social transformations, and focused instead on the specifically *human* environment (cf. 1895: 138).

19. Durkheim acknowledged an overemphasis in *The Division of Labor* on physical density as the "exact expression" of dynamic density, but adds that such an equivalence is surely justified when dealing with the *economic* effects of the latter (cf. 1895: 146 n.21).

20. This restrictive emphasis on the search for concomitant rather than antecedent causes again reflects the deeply uniformitarian conception of social evolution held by Durkheim (cf. 1895: 139–140).

society itself. Moreover, the inner social environment alone can account for the undeniable diversity and complexity of "useful" social facts without recourse to rather arbitrary and *ad hoc* causal hypotheses; and this again indicates the extent to which the *constitution* of qualitatively distinct social types is connected to their *explanation* by a variety of concomitant conditions (1895: 141).

The rules thus established enabled Durkheim aptly to characterize his own conception of collective life by contrast with those of Hobbes and Rousseau, on the one hand, and Spencer, on the other. The first two thinkers viewed the individual as "real" and society as artificial, the latter being imposed upon the former in order to secure certain collective advantages.[21] Spencer, by contrast, viewed society as natural because it expressed certain tendencies of individual human nature, and thus its imposition by force represented an abnormal condition. Durkheim's own theory, as we have seen, contains elements of both—he agreed with Hobbes and Rousseau that constraint is an essential feature of social facts, and with Spencer that society is a part of nature. But precisely because the constraint of society is the consequence of its natural superiority, there is no need to resort to Hobbes's or Rousseau's "social contract" in order to explain the individual's subservience; and inversely, precisely because this natural superiority derives not from Spencer's individual, but from a social reality *sui generis*, the constraint it exercises is not merely physical, but also moral and intellectual. It is that superiority of which religion provided the earliest, symbolic representation, and science the later, more exact explanation.[22]

RULES FOR THE DEMONSTRATION OF SOCIOLOGICAL PROOF

How, then, can we demonstrate that one phenomenon is the cause of another? According to Durkheim, we can only compare those cases where both are simultaneously present (or absent), and ask whether the variations they display in these different circumstances suggest that one depends upon the other. Where the two phenomena are produced artificially by the observer, we call this method

21. This, of course, is a gross distortion of Rousseau; but it is apparently what Durkheim believed.

22. This became a central idea of *The Elementary Forms of the Religious Life* (1912); cf. Durkheim (1895: 143–144) and Chapter 5 below.

experimentation; and where the artificial production of phenomena is impossible, we compare them as they have been produced naturally, a procedure called *indirect experimentation*, or the *comparative method*. Durkheim was convinced that sociology was limited solely to the latter method, and this led him to reject both Comte's "historical" method, which depended on an acceptance of his tendentious "laws" of social progress, and Mill's suggestion that even "indirect" experimentation is inapplicable to the study of social phenomena. In particular, Durkheim attacked Mill's postulate that the same effect can result from various causes as one which would render the scientific analysis of such causes utterly intractable. As the first rule for the demonstration of sociological proof, therefore, Durkheim proposed: *To the same effect there always corresponds the same cause.*[23]

But not all forms of the comparative method, Durkheim argued, are equally applicable to the study of social facts, a view which led him to a critique of the five canons of experimental inquiry contained in Mill's *System of Logic* (1843). Mill's "Method of Agreement," for example, had stated that, if two instances of a phenomenon share only one circumstance, it is either their cause or their effect; his "Method of Difference," by contrast, suggested that, if an instance in which a phenomenon occurs and one in which it does not differ in only one other circumstance, it is the cause, or the effect, or an indispensable part of the cause, of the phenomenon; and his "Joint Method of Agreement and Difference" consisted in combining the first two, putting together knowledge of what is common to all cases of the phenomenon and what alone differs when it is absent. To all three, Durkheim objected on the ground that they assume the cases compared either agree or differ on only one point, conditions difficult enough to achieve in physics, chemistry, and biology, but literally impossible in the study of phenomena as complex as those of sociology. Mill's "Method of Residues" suggested that we subtract from a phenomenon what is known already to be the effect of certain causes, the "residue" being the effect of the remaining antecedents;

23. This principle had already been applied in *The Division of Labor*, where Durkheim insisted that punishment appeared to be the result of various causes only because we have failed to perceive the common element—i.e., the offense done to strong, well-defined states of the *conscience collective*—in its antecedents (cf. 1893: 96–105). The same principle could also be applied in precisely the reverse manner; thus, where suicide was seen to depend on more than one cause, Durkheim insisted that there were in fact several kinds of suicide (cf. 1897b: 145–148).

but here again, Durkheim objected to the assumption that a considerable number of causal laws are already known, and that the effects of all causes but one might thus be eliminated in a science so complex as sociology.

Mill's fifth canon, however, was that of "Concomitant Variation"—that phenomena which vary together are connected through some fact of causation. And this search for a "mere parallelism in values" through which two phenomena pass survived all of Durkheim's objections to the first four. For the manner in which a phenomenon develops reveals its internal nature, and where two phenomena develop in the same way, there must thus be some internal connection between the natures thus revealed. Durkheim could thus do quite well without those massive collections of facts assembled by historians, ethnographers, and sociologists pursuing the "Method of Agreement and Differences." Concomitant variation alone, as long as the variations were serial and systematic rather than isolated and sporadic, was always sufficient to establish a sociological law.[24]

Durkheim then proposed three methods by which such serial, systematic variations might be formed. First, when dealing with very general facts (e.g., suicide) about which we have extensive statistical data,[25] the sociologist might limit his study to a single, unique society. But a second method—i.e., collecting facts from several societies of the same social type—makes available a more extensive field of comparison. The sociologist could now confront the history of one society with another, to see if the same phenomenon evolves over time in response to the same conditions. But this method is applicable only to phenomena which have arisen during the existence of the societies in question, and thus ignores that part of a society's social organization which is inherited ready-made from earlier societies.

This observation led directly to Durkheim's third method: "to account for a social institution belonging to a species already

24. Durkheim was aware, of course, that such laws required interpretation, as in the not infrequent case (some found in *Suicide*) where concomitant variation occurs not because one phenomenon is the cause of another, but because both are the effect of a third; but this, Durkheim observed, is true of any method, and merely imposes certain rules of methodical interpretation (cf. 1895: 152–153).

25. Even here, the fact must be widely prevalent throughout the society while simultaneously varying from region to region; for otherwise, the comparison yields only two parallel curves, one expressing development of the fact under study and the other its hypothesized cause—interesting, but hardly proof (cf. 1895: 156).

determined, we shall compare the different forms which it assumes, not only among peoples of that species, but in all previous species" (1895: 157). This "genetic" method, Durkheim argued, simultaneously yields both an analysis and a synthesis of the facts under study—by showing us how each component element of the phenomenon was successively added to the other, it reveals them in their dissociated state; and by means of the broad field of comparison, the fundamental conditions on which the formation and association of these elements depend are determined. *Consequently, one cannot explain a social fact of any complexity save on condition that one follows its entire development throughout all species.* In so far as it ceases to be purely descriptive and attempts to explain social facts, therefore, comparative sociology is not a single branch of sociology, but is coextensive with the discipline itself.

Finally, Durkheim warned against an error characteristic of such extended comparisons—i.e., in attempting to judge the direction of social evolution, the sociologist compares the state of a social fact during the decline of one society with its state during the early stages of its successor. But the new society, Durkheim insisted, is not simply a continuation of the old; thus, the "revival" of religious traditionalism frequently observed at the outset of a society's history, for example, is the product of the special conditions of that early stage rather than evidence of the "transitoriness" of the religious decline found in the latter stages of its predecessor. To serve as proof, therefore, the comparison of social facts must control for the stage of a society's evolution; and for this purpose, Durkheim concluded, *it will be sufficient to consider societies which one is comparing at the same period of their development*: "According to whether, from one of these stages to the next, it displays more, less, or as much intensity, one will be able to state whether it is progressing, regressing, or remaining static" (1895: 158).

When Durkheim came to summarize the principal characteristics of sociological method, he mentioned three in particular. First, it is independent of all "doctrines," whether philosophical or practical. Sociology is thus neither positivist, nor evolutionist, nor spiritualist, nor even naturalist in so far as that term is taken in the doctrinal sense, as implying the reduction of social facts to cosmic forces; neither has it to take sides on metaphysics, nor affirm free will rather than determinism (or the reverse). Concentrating the last, its only condition is that social facts are explicable by natural causes, a condition that Durkheim regarded less as a rational necessity than a legitimate inductive inference.[26] Similarly, practical doctrines, whether communist, socialist, or individualist, have no scientific value, and if they interest the sociologist at all it is because they are themselves social facts reflective of the interests and desires of certain groups in the society under study.[27]

Second, sociological method is objective, in the sense that social facts are *things* and must be treated as such. This means that we can no longer dream of explaining them by their "utility" or by conscious "reasoning" on the part of their agents; on the contrary, social facts are externally coercive forces, which can be engendered only by other forces: "Thus, to account for social facts, we investigate the forces capable of producing them" (1895: 161).

Finally, these "things" are pre-eminently social things, and Durkheim's method was thus exclusively sociological. A social fact cannot be explained except by another social fact, which to Durkheim meant that the "inner social environment" is the primary motive force underlying all social evolution. Indeed, the sense of this "specific nature of social reality" is so important to the sociologist, Durkheim argued, that a "purely sociological culture," an autonomous scientific discipline, is essential to its cultivation. Three years later *l'Année sociologique* was born.

CRITICAL REMARKS

As Steven Lukes has observed (1972: 226), *The Rules of Sociological Method* was simultaneously a treatise on the philosophy of social science, a polemic against the enemies of sociology, and the manifesto of the emergent Durkheim "School"; and it is important to weigh its failures in the light of these multiple, discordant intentions. Nonetheless, it is difficult to avoid the conclusion that this is Durkheim at his worst, and that he is at his best when, where, to

26. This should not be taken as a claim that sociology and philosophy are of no reciprocal value. On the contrary, some of Durkheim's most important works are efforts to show how sociology, once firmly distinguished from philosophy, might in turn illuminate some of the oldest philosophical dilemmas.

27. Again, it scarcely needs to be added that this is not to say that sociology has no practical value; on the contrary, *all* of Durkheim's sociology was motivated by practical social problems. But scientific solutions to these problems, he insisted, would be forthcoming only when sociologists liberated themselves from doctrinal parties and studied social facts as things.

precisely the extent, and even "because" he departed from these programmatic utterances. The concept of the "social fact" itself, for example, must be described as extraordinarily capacious if not downright indiscriminate, incorporating the full range of potentially explanatory social phenomena—population size and distribution, social norms and rules, collective beliefs and practices, currents of opinion—from the infrastructural to the superstructural level; and as Durkheim's willingness to focus on the latter rather than the former increased over the course of his career, *The Rules*— rather awkwardly for so imperious a piece—appeared to straddle an equivocal, intermediate stage.[28]

It might be argued, of course, that these ambiguities are somewhat relieved by Durkheim's insistence that social facts may be distinguished from their biological and psychological counterparts by their "externality" and powers of "constraint"; but here similar difficulties persist. The suggestion that social facts are external to any particular individual, for example, raises few objections, though a concern for balanced statement might add (as Durkheim increasingly did) that they are also *internal* to particular individuals; but the suggestion that social facts are external to all individuals can be justified only in the limited sense that they have a prior temporal existence, and any extension beyond these limits is subject (as Durkheim frequently was) to charges of hypostatizing some metaphysical "group mind" (Lukes, 1982: 3–4).

The term "constraint" seems to have enjoyed a still greater elasticity, for Durkheim used it variously to refer to the authority of laws as manifested through repressive sanctions; the need to follow certain rules in order to successfully perform certain tasks; the influence of the structural features of a society on its cultural norms and rules; the psychological pressures of a crowd on its members; and the effect of socialization and acculturation on the individual. The first of these usages, Lukes has observed, seems more felicitous than the second (which is perhaps better described as a "means–end" relation); and the last three seem something else altogether—i.e., far from being cases of "constraint" or "coercion," they rather describe how men are led to think and feel in a certain way, to know and value

28. In *The Division of Labor*, for example, Durkheim criticized Fustel for suggesting that "the primitive family was constituted on a religious base," and thus for mistaking "the cause for the effect" (1893: 179), while his review of Antonio Labriola's *Essais sur la conception materialiste de l'histoire* insisted that from religion "have come all the other manifestations of collective activity..." (1897a: 129).

certain things, and to act accordingly (cf. Lukes, 1982: 4). It was
these latter usages, moreover, which Durkheim increasingly adopted
as his interests shifted from the structural emphases of *The Division
of Labor* to the focus on collective representations characteristic of
The Elementary Forms; as he did so, "constraint" became less an
"essential characteristic" than a "perceptible sign,"[29] and eventually,
it disappeared altogether.

Like his definition of social facts, Durkheim's rules for their
explanation represent a laudable effort to establish sociology as a
science independent of psychology; but here again, "psychology"
seems to have meant several different things to Durkheim—
explanation in terms of "organico-psychic" factors like race and/or
heredity; explanation by "individual and particular" rather than
"social and general" conditions; and, most frequently, explanation in
terms of "individual mental states or dispositions."[30] In each
instance, Durkheim discovered logical or empirical shortcomings; but
if social facts thus cannot be *completely* explained by psychological
facts, it is at least equally true that even the most determinedly
"sociological" explanations necessarily rely upon certain assump-
tions, explicit or otherwise, about how individual human beings
think, feel, and act in particular circumstances. Sociology may not
produce many laws, W.G. Runciman has observed (1983: 32), but it
certainly consumes them—especially those of psychology.[31] Durkheim's insistence that social facts can be explained only by other
social facts was thus both excessive and naive.

Durkheim's effort to find objective criteria by which "normal"
might be distinguished from "pathological" social facts was a rather
transparent attempt to grant scientific status to those social and
political preferences we have already observed in Book Three of *The
Division of Labor*. In addition to the logical difficulties of inferring
"social health" from the "generality" of a phenomenon, Durkheim

29. Cf. the preface to the second edition of *The Rules of Sociological Method* (1901:
47).

30. Quite aside from his attack on psychology as a mode of explanation, Durkheim
frequently described it in terms of its *object*—i.e., the *conscience* and its *représentations*. As his interest in such phenomena increased in his later work, Durkheim
frequently distinguished between "individual psychology," which studies individual
représentations, and "socio-psychology," which studies their collective counterparts;
and though his own interest lay entirely in the latter, he considered both studies
legitimate (cf. Lukes, 1982: 7).

31. Essentially the same point is made independently by Lukes (1982: 17–18).

himself recognized the practical obstacles to drawing such inferences in "transition periods" like his own; but since economic anarchy, anomie, and rapidly rising suicide rates were all "general" features of "organized" societies, Durkheim's second criterion—that this generality be related to the general conditions of the social type in question—could render them "pathological" only by reference to some future, integrated society which Durkheim somehow considered "latent" in the present. Durkheim, in short, tended to idealize future societies while dismissing present realities, and thus appears to have been oblivious to the sheer historical contingency of all social arrangements (Lukes, 1972: 29).[32]

The example chosen to illustrate these criteria—the "normality" of crime—reflects the same conservative preconceptions. Even if we accept the argument that the punishment elicited by crime reaffirms that solidarity based on shared beliefs and sentiments, for example, we must still ask a series of more specific questions—Which beliefs and sentiments? Shared by whom? What degree of punishment? Which "criminal" offenses? Committed by whom? For in the absence of specific answers to such questions (Durkheim's treatment of these issues is unrelievedly abstract), the claim that crime is functional to social integration could be used to justify *any* favored set of beliefs and practices, and *any* type or degree of punishment, simply by arguing that the failure to punish would be followed inevitably by social disintegration. Durkheim's additional claim—that crime is functional to social change—was a simple extension of the view discussed in Chapter 2, that law is the direct reflection of the *conscience collective*. But, as Tarde was quick to point out, there is no *necessary* connection between the violation of these laws constituting crimes and the sources of moral and social innovation.[33]

Taken together, these criticisms suggest that Durkheim's claim that his sociological method was free of philosophical and political doctrines must be considered an instance of what Jürgen Habermas might call his "self-misunderstanding." Philosophically, for example, Durkheim was clearly a social realist and rationalist—he believed that society is a reality independent of individual minds, and that the methodical elimination of our subjective preconceptions will enable

32. It was this utterly conservative perspective which led Durkheim to see sociology as analogous to medicine, and the sociologist as a kind of physician.

33. Cf. Lukes and Scull (1983: 15–19); and Tarde, "Criminality and Social Health" (1895), in Lukes and Scull (1983: 76–92).

us to know it "as it is." In so far as social facts are culturally transmitted from one generation to another, and individuals do learn and are thus shaped by them, this is unobjectionable; but it is equally true that social facts are themselves *constituted* by the meanings attached to them by those agents whose acts, thoughts, and feelings they are, and that such subjective interpretations are thus a part of the reality to be "known." The question of what religion "is," for example, is hardly one which can be settled aside from the meanings attached to it by those whose "religion" is under investigation; and any effort to study it independent of such meanings runs the risk not merely of abstracting some "essentialist" definition of religion bearing no relation to the beliefs and practices in question, but also of unconsciously imposing one's own subjective interpretation under the guise of detached, scientific observation.[34]

Politically, as we have seen, Durkheim maintained that scholars make poor activists, abstained from participation in socialist circles, and generally presented himself as a sociological expert advising his contemporaries on their "true" societal interests; but it is difficult to see how theories which so consistently and emphatically endorsed the secular, democratic, egalitarian, anti-royalist, and anti-revolutionary values of the Third Republic could reasonably be regarded as devoid of political interests and objectives. The point here is not simply that these theories served political ends, or even that these ends were Durkheim's own; it is rather that here the distinction between social thought and social action becomes elusive to the point of non-existence; for Durkheim's entire social science, including choice and formulation of problems, definition of terms, classification of social types, explanatory hypotheses, methods of proof—indeed, even the denial of all philosophical and political commitments itself—was a deeply political act (cf. Lukes, 1982: 22–23).

34. Both risks, of course, are taken repeatedly in *The Elementary Forms of the Religious Life* (1912), with predictable results. See Chapter 5 below.

4

The Social Conditions of Psychological Health: Suicide (1897)

WHAT IS SUICIDE?

Explanation requires comparison; comparison requires classification; classification requires the definition of those facts to be classified, compared, and ultimately explained. Consistent with *The Rules of Sociological Method*, therefore, Durkheim began his 1897 work with a warning against *notiones vulgares*, together with an insistence that

> our first task ... must be to determine the order of facts to be studied under the name of suicide ... we must inquire whether, among the different varieties of death, some have common qualities objective enough to be recognized by all honest observers, specific enough not to be found elsewhere and also sufficiently kin to those commonly called suicides for us to retain the same term without breaking with common usage. (1897b: 42)

Durkheim's initial effort at such a definition indeed followed common usage, according to which a "suicide" is any death which is the immediate or eventual result of a positive (e.g., shooting oneself) or negative (e.g., refusing to eat) act accomplished by the victim himself.[1] But here Durkheim immediately ran into difficulties, for

1. Durkheim recognized that this distinction was already not without ambiguity: "In one sense, few cases of death exist which are not immediately or distantly due to some act of the subject. The causes of death are outside rather than within us, and are effective only if we venture into their sphere of activity" (1897b: 43).

this definition failed to distinguish between two very different sorts of death: the victim of hallucination who leaps from an upper story window while thinking it on a level with the ground; and the sane individual who does the same thing *knowing* that it will lead to his death. The obvious solution—i.e., to restrict the definition of suicide to actions *intended* to have this result—was unacceptable to Durkheim for at least two reasons. First, as we have seen (p. 64 above), Durkheim consistently tried to define social facts by easily ascertainable characteristics, and the intentions of agents were ill-fitted to this purpose. Second, the definition of suicide by the end sought by the agent would exclude actions—e.g., the mother sacrificing herself for her child—in which death is clearly not "sought" but is nonetheless an inevitable consequence of the act in question, and is thus a "suicide" by any other name.

The distinctive characteristic of suicides, therefore, is not that the act is performed *intentionally*, but rather that it is performed *advisedly*—the agent knows that death will be the result of his act, regardless of whether or not death is his goal. This criterion is sufficient to distinguish suicide, properly so-called, from other deaths which are either inflicted on oneself unconsciously or not self-inflicted at all; moreover, Durkheim insisted that such a characteristic was easily ascertainable, and that such acts thus formed a definite, homogeneous group. Hence Durkheim's definition: *Suicide is applied to all cases of death resulting directly or indirectly from a positive or negative act of the victim himself, which he knows will produce this result.*

This definition, however, was subject to two immediate objections. The first was that such foreknowledge is a matter of degree, varying considerably from one person or situation to another. At what point, for example, does the death of a professional dare-devil or that of a man neglectful of his health cease to be an "accident" and start to become "suicide"? But for Durkheim to ask this question was less to raise an objection to his definition than to correctly identify its greatest advantage—that it indicates the place of suicide within moral life as a whole. For suicides, according to Durkheim, do not constitute a wholly distinctive group of "monstrous phenomena" unrelated to other forms of behavior; on the contrary, they are related to other acts, both courageous and imprudent, by an unbroken series of intermediate cases. Suicides, in short, are simply an exaggerated form of common practices.

The second objection was that such practices, however common, are individual practices, with individual causes and consequences, which are thus the proper subject matter of psychology rather than sociology. In fact, Durkheim never denied that suicide could be studied by the methods of psychology, but he did insist that suicide could also be studied independent of its individual manifestations, as a social fact *sui generis*. Indeed, each society has a "definite aptitude" for suicide, the relative intensity of which can be measured by the proportion of suicides per total population, or what Durkheim called "the rate of mortality through suicide, characteristic of the society under consideration" (1897b: 48). This rate, Durkheim insisted, was both permanent (the rate for any individual society was less variable than that of most other leading demographic data, including the general mortality rate) and variable (the rate for each society was sufficiently peculiar to that society as to be more characteristic of it than its general mortality rate); and, just as the first would be inexplicable were it not "the result of a group of distinct character- istics, solidary with one another, and simultaneously effective in spite of different attendant circumstances," so the second proved "the concrete and individual quality of these same characteristics, since they vary with the individual character of society itself" (1897b: 51). Each society, Durkheim thus concluded, is predisposed to contribute a definite quota of suicides; and it was this predisposition[2] which Durkheim proposed to study sociologically.

Thus defined, Durkheim's project again fell naturally into three parts: first, an examination of those extra-social causes sufficiently general to have a possible effect on the social suicide rate (but which in fact influence it little, if at all); second, the determination of the nature of the social causes, the way in which they produce their effects, and their relations to those individual conditions normally associated with the different kinds of suicide; and third, the more precise account of the "suicide aptitude" described above, of its relation to other social facts, and of the means by which this collective tendency might be counteracted.

2. Durkheim did not deny, therefore, that individual conditions may cause individual suicides, nor did he deny that this was a profitable area of study for psychologists; but most of these conditions are insufficiently general to affect the suicide rate of the society as a whole, and thus they were of no interest to the sociologist (cf. 1897b: 51–52).

EXTRA-SOCIAL CAUSES

Durkheim suggested that, *a priori*, there are two kinds of extra-social causes sufficiently general to have an influence on the suicide rate. First, within the individual psychological constitution there might exist an inclination, normal or pathological, varying from country to country, which directly leads people to commit suicide. Second, the nature of the external physical environment (climate, temperature, etc.) might indirectly have the same effect. Durkheim took up each in turn.

The annual rate of certain diseases, like the suicide rate, is both relatively stable for a given society and perceptibly variable from one society to another; and since insanity is such a disease, the demonstration that suicide is the consequence of insanity (a psychological fact) would successfully account for those features of permanence and variability which had led Durkheim to suggest that suicide was a social fact *sui generis*. Durkheim was thus particularly concerned to eliminate insanity as a probable cause of suicide, and he did so by attacking that hypothesis in its two most common forms: the view that suicide itself is a special form of insanity, and the view that suicide is simply an effect of various types of insanity. The first Durkheim dismissed by classifying suicidal insanity as a "mono-mania"—a form of mental illness limited to a single act or object—and then arguing that not a single incontestable example of such monomania had yet been shown to exist. The second he rejected on the ground that all suicides committed by the insane are either devoid of deliberation and motive altogether or based on motives that are purely hallucinatory, while many suicides are "doubly identifiable as being deliberate and springing from representations involved in this deliberation which are not purely hallucinatory" (1897b: 67). There are many suicides, therefore, not connected with insanity.

But what about psychopathic conditions which fall short of insanity—neurasthenia and alcoholism—but which nonetheless are frequently associated with suicide? Durkheim responded by showing that the social suicide rate bears no definite relation to that of neurasthenia, and that the latter thus has no necessary effect on the former; and alcoholism was discarded as a putative cause on evidence that the geographical distributions of both alcohol consumption and prosecutions for alcoholism bear no relation to that of suicides. A psychopathic state, Durkheim concluded, may predispose individuals to commit suicide, but it is never in itself a sufficient cause of the permanence and variability of suicide rates.

Having dismissed pathological states as a class of causes, Durkheim turned his attention to those normal psychological conditions (race and heredity), which, again, are sufficiently general to account for the phenomena in question. The view that suicide is the consequence of tendencies inherent in each major social type, for example, was undermined by the enormous variations in social suicide rates observed *within* the same type, suggesting that different levels of civilization are much more decisive. But the argument that suicide is hereditary had first to be distinguished from the more moderate view that one inherits a predisposition to commit suicide; for the latter, as in the case of neurasthenia, is not an "explanation" of suicide at all. The stronger argument—that one inherits a semi-autonomous psychological mechanism which gives rise to suicide automatically— was then rejected on the grounds that its most dramatic manifestation (the regularity with which suicide sometimes appears in the same family) can be explained by other causes (contagion), and that, as within racial types, there are patterned variations *within* the same family (between husbands and wives) which, on this hypothesis, would be rendered inexplicable.

But if normal or abnormal psychological predispositions are not, by themselves, sufficient causes of suicide, might not such predispositions acting in concert with cosmic factors (climate, seasonal temperature, etc.) have such a determinative effect? The conjunction of such predispositions with climate, Durkheim answered, has no such influence; for, while the geographical distribution of suicides in Europe varies according to latitude and thus roughly according to climate as well, these variations are better explained by social causes. Montesquieu's suggestion that cold, foggy countries are most favorable to suicide was equally discredited by the fact that, in every country for which statistics were available, the suicide rate is higher in spring and summer than in fall and winter.

Is suicide, then, as the Italian statisticians Ferri and Morselli believed, an effect of the mechanical influence of heat on the cerebral functions? Durkheim here objected on both conceptual and empirical grounds—that this theory presumes that the constant psychological antecedent of suicide is a state of extreme excitation, where in fact it is frequently preceded by depression; and, in any case, that the suicide rate is in decline in July and August, and thus does not vary regularly with temperature. The "revised" Italian argument—that it is the *contrast* between the departing cold and the beginning of the warm season that stimulates the psychological predispositions—was equally rejected by Durkheim as inconsistent with the perfect continuity (steady increase from January to June, steady decrease from July to December) of the curve representing the monthly variations of the suicide rate.

Consistent with the argument of *The Rules* (Chapter VI), Durkheim insisted that such a perfectly continuous variation could be explained only by causes themselves varying with the same continuity; and, as a first clue to the nature of these causes, he pointed out that the proportional share of each month in the total number of annual suicides is perfectly parallel with the average length of the day at the same time of the year. Other clues follow: suicide is more common by day than by night, in morning and afternoon than at midday, and on weekdays than on weekends (except for an increase of female suicides on Sundays). In every case, Durkheim observed, suicide increases in those months, days of the week, and hours of the day when social life is most active, and decreases when collective activity declines. Anticipating the argument of Book Two, Durkheim thus suggested that suicide is the consequence of the intensity of social life; but before he could proceed to explain *how* such a cause might produce such an effect, Durkheim had to deal with one other "psychological" theory—Tarde's argument that social facts in general, and suicide in particular, can be explained as the consequence of *imitation.*

The term "imitation," Durkheim began, is used indiscriminately to explain three very different groups of facts: (1) that complex process whereby individual states of consciousness act and react upon one another in such a way as to produce a new, collective state *sui generis*; (2) that impulse which leads us to conform to the manners, customs, and moral practices of our societies; and (3) that largely unpremeditated, automatic reproduction of actions just because they have occurred in our presence or we have heard of them. The first, Durkheim insisted, can hardly be called "imitation," for it involves no act of genuine reproduction whatsoever;[3] the second involves an

3. It is interesting to see how little Durkheim claimed to understand this process in 1897 (cf. 1897b: 125–127, 130 n. 10), particularly in light of its significance in Durkheim's later explanation of religious belief and ritual (cf. 1912: 240–245).

act of reproduction, but one inspired both by the specific nature of the manners, customs, and practices in question, and by the specific feelings of respect or sympathy they inspire, and thus one ill-described by the term "imitation"; only in the third case, where the act is a mere echo of the original, and subject to no cause outside of itself, is the term warranted. Hence Durkheim's definition: *"Imitation exists when the immediate antecedent of an act is the representation of a like act, previously performed by someone else; with no explicit or implicit mental operation which bears upon the intrinsic nature of the act reproduced intervening between representation and execution"* (1897b: 129).

Thus defined, of course, imitation is reduced to a purely psychological phenomenon; for while the synthesis of individual consciousnesses into a collective state *sui generis* and conformity to obligatory beliefs and practices are both highly social, "imitation properly so-called" is mere repetition, creating no intellectual or moral bond between its agent and his antecedent. We imitate other human beings in the same way that we reproduce the sounds of nature, physical objects, or the movements of non-human animals; and since no clearly social element is involved in the latter, neither is there such an element in the former. To suggest that the suicide rate might be explained by imitation, therefore, was to suggest that a social fact might be explained by a psychological fact—a possibility Durkheim had already denied in *The Rules*.

Durkheim's definition[4] clearly reduced the number of suicides attributable to imitation. But it did not eliminate them; on the contrary, Durkheim insisted that there was no other phenomenon so "contagious" as suicide. But it did not follow that this contagious quality necessarily had social consequences—affected the social suicide rate—for its consequences might instead be merely individual and sporadic; and if imitation did *not* affect the suicide rate, it was doubtful (*pace* Tarde) that it had any social consequences whatso-

---

4. Durkheim also distinguished between suicides caused by moral *contagion* (originating in one or two individual cases and then repeated by others) and those caused by moral *epidemic* (originating in the whole group under the influence of a common pressure); the first involved imitation and were thus attributable to psychological causes, while the second was a social fact subject to social causes (cf. 1897b: 131–132).

ever, for no phenomenon was more affected by imitation than suicide.[5]

If, on the other hand, imitation *does* influence suicide rates, Durkheim suggested, this should be reflected in the geographical distribution of suicides—the rate typical of one country should be transmitted to its neighbors; and, indeed, contiguous geographical areas do reveal similar suicide rates. But such a geographical "diffusion" of suicides might equally well be explained by the parallel "diffusion" of distinctively *social* influences throughout the same region. In addition to similarity of rates in geographically contiguous areas, therefore, the "imitation hypothesis" further requires that there be a "model" of particularly intense suicidal activity, and that this activity be "visible" enough to fulfill its function as a model to be imitated. These conditions are in fact fulfilled by the major urban centers in western European countries; thus, we ought to expect the geographical distribution of suicides to reveal a pattern of concentration around major cities, with concentric circles of gradually less intensive suicidal activity radiating out into the countryside. Instead, we find suicide occurring in roughly homogeneous masses over broad regions with no central nuclei, an observation which suggests not only the complete absence of any local influence of imitation, but the presence of the much more general causes of the social environment. Most decisive, however, is the fact that an abrupt change in that social environment is accompanied by an equally abrupt change in the suicide rate, one which is not reflected beyond the bounds of the social environment in question, and thus one which could hardly be explained as the consequence of imitation.

But Durkheim's argument in fact went much further than this denial that, its individual effects notwithstanding, imitation is an insufficient cause for variations in the suicide rate; for, in addition, he insisted that imitation alone has no effect on suicide whatsoever. This extension of his argument was the consequence of Durkheim's more general theoretical commitment to the view that the thought of an act is never sufficient to produce the act itself unless the person thinking is already so disposed; and the dispositions in question, of course, are

5. This seems to have been the main point of this chapter altogether; cf. Durkheim's conclusion: "No fact is more readily transmissible by contagion than suicide, yet we have just seen that this contagiousness has no social effects. If imitation is so much without social influence in this case, it cannot have more in others; the virtues ascribed to it are therefore imaginary" (1897b: 141–142).

the result of social causes. Imitation, therefore, is not a real cause, even of individual suicides: "It only exposes a state which is the true generating cause of the act," Durkheim concluded, "and which probably would have produced its natural effect even had imitation not intervened, for the predisposition must be very strong to enable so slight a matter to translate it into action" (1897b: 141).

SOCIAL CAUSES AND SOCIAL TYPES

Durkheim's argument so far is a perfect example of his character-istic "argument by elimination" — the systematic rejection of alternative explanations of a given phenomenon in order to lend authority to the "sole remaining" candidate (cf. Lukes, 1972: 31–32). He thus claimed to have shown that, for each social group, there is a specific tendency to suicide that can be explained neither by the "organic-psychic constitution" of individuals nor by the nature of the physical environment; and as his discussion of geographic and seasonal variations of suicide has already hinted, the tendency in question must thus be, in itself, a collective phenomenon, and must depend upon social causes.

But is there, in fact, one "single, indestructible" suicidal tendency? Or are there rather several, which should be distinguished from one another and then studied separately? Durkheim had already pon-dered this difficulty in Book One, in his discussion of suicide by insanity; and his solution there was repeated here. Briefly, the suicidal tendency, single or not, is observable only in its individual manifestations (individual suicides); thus, Durkheim proposed to classify suicides into distinct "types" or "species" according to their similarities and differences, on the assumption that there would be as many types as there were suicides having the same essential characteristics, and as many "tendencies" as there were types.

This solution, however, immediately raised another problem. In his treatment of suicides by insanity, Durkheim had at his disposal many good descriptions of individual cases—of the agent's psycho-logical state prior to the act, of his preparations to commit the act, of the manner in which the act was performed, etc. But such data were almost completely unavailable for suicides committed by sane people, a fact which rendered classification by external manifesta-tions impossible. Durkheim was thus forced to alter his strategy—

indeed, to "reverse the order of study" altogether, adopting an "aetiological" rather than "morphological" system of classification. Assuming, as always, that any given effect has one, and only one, corresponding cause, Durkheim argued that there must be as many special types of suicide as there are special causes producing them: "Without asking why [these types of suicide] differ from one another," Durkheim proposed, "we will first seek the social conditions responsible for them; [we will] then group these conditions in a number of separate classes by their resemblances and differences, and we shall be sure that a specific type of suicide will correspond to each of these classes" (1897b: 147).

How, then, do we determine the *causes* of suicide? One answer was simply to rely on statistical records of the "presumptive motive of suicide" (apparently construed as a cause) kept by officials in most modern societies; but, despite its obvious convenience and plausibility, Durkheim rejected this resource for at least two reasons. First, such "statistics of the motives of suicides" were actually statistics of officials' *opinions* of such motives, which thus embodied not only difficult assessments of material fact, but still more difficult explanations and evaluations of actions performed at will. Second, regardless of the credibility of such reports, Durkheim simply denied that motives were true causes, a characteristic position he supported by pointing to the contrast between relatively constant proportions of different classes of "motive explanations" (both over time and across occupational groups) and extremely variable suicide rates themselves (over the same time period and across the same occupational groups). These "reasons" to which suicides are ascribed, Durkheim thus insisted, are only apparent causes, individual repercussions of more general states which they only imperfectly express: "They may be said to indicate the individual's weak points, where the outside current bearing the impulse to self-destruction most easily finds introduction. But they are no part of this current itself, and consequently cannot help us to understand it" (1897b: 151). Disregarding such individual repercussions, therefore, Durkheim turned directly to the "states of the various social environments" (religious confessions, familial and political society, occupational groups) across which the variations in suicide rates occur, and within which their causes might be found.

Egoistic Suicide

Durkheim first asked how the different religious confessions affect suicide. If we look at a map of Western Europe, for example, we see that where Protestants are most numerous the suicide rate is highest, that where Catholics predominate it is much lower, and that the aptitude of Jews for suicide is lower still, though to a lesser degree, than that of Catholics. How are these data to be explained?

Again, Durkheim escorted the reader through an argument by elimination. In many of the societies under observation, for example, Jews and Catholics are less numerous than Protestants; thus it it tempting to explain their lower suicide rates as the consequence of that rigorous moral discipline which religious minorities sometimes impose upon themselves in the face of the hostility of surrounding populations. But such an explanation, Durkheim observed, ignores at least three facts: first, suicide is too little an object of public condemnation for religious hostility to have this effect: second, religious hostility frequently produces not the moral conformity of those against whom it is directed, but rather their rebellion against it; and third, the reduced suicide rate of Catholics relative to Protestants is independent of their minority status—even in Spain, Catholics commit suicide less frequently.

The last point in particular suggested an alternative explanation— that the cause for lower rates of suicide is to be found within the nature of the religious confession itself. But such an explanation, Durkheim insisted, cannot refer to the religious *percepts* of the confession, for there Catholics and Protestants prohibit suicide with equal emphasis; rather, the explanation must proceed from one of the more general characteristics differentiating them, and that characteristic—indeed, "the only essential difference between Catholicism and Protestantism"—is that the latter permits free inquiry to a greater degree than the former (1897b: 157).[6]

But if the proclivity of Protestantism for suicide must thus be related to its spirit of free inquiry, this "free inquiry" itself requires explanation, for it brings as much sorrow as happiness, and thus is not "intrinsically desirable." Why, then, do men seek and even demand

6. Here Durkheim was not denying the *idealistic* nature of Roman Catholicism by contrast, for example, with Greco-Latin polytheism and Hebrew monotheism; rather, he was arguing that Protestantism stresses religious individualism and freedom of personal interpretation, while "all variation is abhorrent to Catholic thought" (1897b: 158).

such freedom? Durkheim's answer: "Reflection develops only if its development becomes imperative, that is, if certain ideas and instinctive sentiments which have hitherto adequately guided conduct are found to have lost their efficacy. Then reflection intervenes to fill the gap that has appeared, but which it has not created" (1897b: 158). In other words, Protestantism concedes greater freedom of thought to the individual because it has fewer commonly accepted beliefs and practices. Indeed, as we have already seen in Chapter 2, it was this possession of a common, collective credo that, for Durkheim, was the essence of religious society itself, and that distinguished it from those merely temporal bonds which unite men through the exchange and reciprocity of services, yet permit and even presuppose differences; and, precisely to the extent that Protestantism lacked such a credo, it was a less strongly integrated church than its Roman Catholic counterpart.

Durkheim then suggested that this explanation is consistent with at least three other observations. First, it would account for the still lower suicide rates of Jews who, in response to the hostility[7] directed against them, established strong community ties of thought and action, virtually eliminated individual divergences, and thus achieved a high degree of unity, solidarity, and integration. Second, of all the great Protestant countries, England has the lowest suicide rate; and it also has the most "integrated" of Protestant churches. And third, since knowledge is the natural consequence of free inquiry, we should expect that suicide increases with its acquisition, and Durkheim had little trouble demonstrating that this was the case.

But this last demonstration did raise an anomaly: the Jews, who are both highly educated and have low suicide rates. But for Durkheim, this was the proverbial exception that proves the rule. For the Jew seeks to learn, not in order to replace traditional beliefs with individual reflection, but rather to protect himself from others' hostility through his superior knowledge. "So the exception," Durkheim observed, "is only apparent;"

> it even confirms the law. Indeed, it proves that if the suicidal tendency is great in educated circles, this is due, as we have said, to the weakening of traditional beliefs and to the state of moral individualism

---

7. Durkheim thus acknowledged the role of minority status, not because religious hostility imposes some "higher morality," but because it forces the minority to achieve greater unity and integration (cf. 1897b: 159–160).

resulting from this; for it disappears when education has another cause and responds to other needs. (1897b: 168)

Finally, it should be noted that the combined effect of these observations on religious confessions and suicide was an implicit celebration of the Third Republic in general and its program of secular education in particular. For, as Durkheim was pleased to make clear, the long-acknowledged correlation between the growth of knowledge and suicide could not be taken to mean that the former "causes" the latter; on the contrary, knowledge and suicide are independent effects of a more general cause—the decline of traditional beliefs. Moreover, once these beliefs have declined, they cannot be artificially reestablished,[8] and thus free inquiry and the knowledge that results become our only resources in the effort to replace them. Finally, Durkheim had shown that the prophylactic effect of religion on suicide owed little to its condemnation of suicide, its idea of God, or its promise of a future life; rather, religion protects man from suicide "because it is a society. What constitutes this society is the existence of a certain number of beliefs and practices common to all the faithful, traditional and thus obligatory. The more numerous and strong these collective states of mind are," Durkheim concluded, "the stronger the integration of the religious community, and also the greater its preservative value" (1897b: 170).

But if religion thus preserves men from suicide because it is a society, other "societies" (e.g., the family and political society) ought to have the same effect. After developing a statistical measure of the immunity to suicide enjoyed by various groups,[9] for example, Durkheim was able to show that, while marriage alone has a preservative effect against suicide, this is limited and benefits only men; the larger family unit, on the other hand, provides an immunity which husband and wife share. Similarly, when one marital partner dies, the survivor loses a degree of suicidal immunity; but this loss is less a consequence of the severing of the conjugal bond alone than of

8. Cf. the similar point in *The Division of Labor* (1893: 409).

9. This was Durkheim's famous "coefficient of preservation"—the number showing how many times less frequent suicide is in one group than in another at the same age. Thus, when Durkheim said that the coefficient of preservation of husbands of the age of 25 in relation to unmarried men is 3, he meant that, if the tendency to suicide of married persons at this time of life is represented by 1, that of unmarried persons must be represented by 3. When the coefficient of preservation sinks below 1, Durkheim described it as a "coefficient of aggravation" (1897b: 177).

the more general shock to the family that the survivor must endure. Finally, the immunity to suicide increases with the size of the family,[10] a fact Durkheim attributed to the greater number and intensity of collective sentiments produced and repeatedly reinforced by the larger group.

Similarly, the examination of political societies showed that suicide, quite rare in a society's early stages, increases as that society matures and disintegrates. During social disturbances or great popular wars, by contrast, the suicide rate declines, a fact that Durkheim claimed is susceptible of only one interpretation—that these disturbances "rouse collective sentiments, stimulate partisan spirit and patriotism, political and national faith alike, and, concentrating activity toward a single end, at least temporarily cause a stronger integration of society" (1897b: 208)

Suicide thus varies inversely with the degree of integration of the religious, domestic, and political groups of which the individual forms a part; in short, as a society weakens or "disintegrates," the individual depends less on the group, depends more upon himself, and recognizes no rules of conduct beyond those based upon private interests. Durkheim called this state of "excessive individualism" *egoism*, and the special type of self-inflicted death it produces *egoistic suicide*.

But why does individualism thus cause suicide? The traditional view—that man, by his psychological nature, cannot live without some transcendent, eternal reason beyond this life—was rejected on the ground that, were our desire for immortality so great, nothing in this life could satisfy us; whereas, in fact, we do take pleasure in our temporal lives, and the pleasures we take are not merely physical and individual, but also moral and social, both in their origin and in their purpose. Durkheim thus returned to the conception of the duality of human nature first found in *The Division of Labor*:

> . . . social man superimposes himself upon physical man. Social man necessarily presupposes a society which he expresses or serves. If this dissolves, if we can no longer feel it in existence and action about and above us, whatever is social in us is deprived of all objective

10. Durkheim thus rejected the Malthusian connection between limitation of family size and general well-being: "Actually [this restriction] is so much a source of the reverse condition that it diminishes the human desire to live. Far from dense families being a sort of unnecessary luxury appropriate only to the rich, they are actually an indispensable staff of daily life" (1897b: 201).

foundation .... Thus we are bereft of reasons for existence; for the only life to which we could cling no longer corresponds to anything actual; the only existence still based upon reality no longer meets our needs .... So there is nothing more for our efforts to lay hold of, and we feel them lose themselves in emptiness. (1897b: 213)

It is in this social (rather than the earlier, psychological) sense, therefore, that our activity needs an object transcending it; for such an object is implicit within our moral constitution itself, and cannot be lost without this constitution losing its *raison d'être* to the same degree. In this state of moral confusion, the least cause of discouragement gives birth to desperate, self-destructive resolutions, a suicidal tendency that infects not only individuals but whole societies; and, precisely because these intellectual currents *are* collective, they impose their authority on the individual and drive him even further in the direction he is already, by internal disposition, inclined to go. Ironically, therefore, the individual submits to the influence of society at the very moment that he frees himself from it: "However individualized a man may be, there is always something collective remaining—the very depression and melancholy resulting from this same exaggerated individualism" (1897b: 214).

Altruistic Suicide

But if excessive individuation thus leads to suicide, so does insufficient individuation; thus, among primitive peoples, we find several categories of suicide—men on the threshold of old age, women upon the deaths of their husbands, followers and servants upon the deaths of their chiefs—in which the person kills himself *because it is his duty*. Such a sacrifice, Durkheim argued, is imposed by society for social purposes; and for society to be able to do this, the individual personality must have little value, a state Durkheim called *altruism*, and whose corresponding mode of self-inflicted death was called *obligatory altruistic suicide*.[11]

11. "Obligatory" altruistic suicide is the essential type, from which two others derive—i.e., "optional" altruistic suicide, in which a concurrence of circumstances makes self-inflicted death praiseworthy, thus encouraging it without requiring it; and "acute" altruistic suicide (of which "mystical" suicide is the "perfect pattern"), in which the individual kills himself for the pure joy of sacrifice and self-renunciation (cf. 1897b: 222–225).

Like all suicides, the altruist kills himself because he is unhappy;[12] but this unhappiness is distinctive both in its causes and in its effects. While the egoist is unhappy because he sees nothing "real" in the world besides the individual, for example, the altruist is sad because the individual seems so "unreal"; the egoist sees no goal to which he might commit himself, and thus feels useless and without purpose, while the altruist commits himself to a goal beyond this world, and henceforth this world is an obstacle and burden to him. The melancholy of the egoist is one of incurable weariness and sad depression, and is expressed in a complete relaxation of all activity; the unhappiness of the altruist, by contrast, springs from hope, faith, even enthusiasm, and affirms itself in acts of extraordinary energy.

Altruistic suicide thus reflects that crude morality which disregards the individual, while its egoistic counterpart elevates the human personality beyond collective constraints; and their differences thus correspond to those between primitive and advanced societies. But altruistic suicides do occur among more civilized peoples—among the early Christian martyrs and the French revolutionaries—and in contemporary French society, Durkheim insisted, there even exists a "special environment" in which altruistic suicide is chronic: the army. Military suicide thus represents an evolutionary survival of the morality of primitive peoples: "Influenced by this predisposition," Durkheim observed, "the soldier kills himself at the least disappointment, for the most futile reasons, for a refusal of leave, a reprimand, an unjust punishment, a delay in promotion, a question of honor, a flush of momentary jealousy, or even simply because other suicides have occurred before his eyes or to his knowledge" (1897b: 238–239). The "contagious" suicides ascribed by Tarde to psychological causes, Durkheim thus insisted, are rather explained by the moral constitution which predisposes men to imitate one another's actions.

Finally, Durkheim's discussion of altruistic suicide aptly illustrates some of the most characteristic arguments of the work as a whole—his rejection of any definition of suicide which appeals to subjective mental states (motives, purposes, etc.), his suggestion that self-inflicted deaths reflect the most general moral sentiments of the societies within which they occur, and the view that such suicides are

12. This is not to say that a melancholy view of life automatically increases the inclination to suicide. Christians, for example, have a gloomy conception of this life combined with an aversion to suicide, a conjunction Durkheim attributed to their "moderate individualism" (cf. 1897b: 226).

thus merely exaggerated expressions of behavior which, in more moderated form, would be labeled "virtuous." However pure the motives which led to the "heroic" suicide of Cato, for example, it was not different *in kind* from that of one of Frazer's primitive Polynesian chiefs; and where altruistic suicides reflect a courageous indifference to the loss of one's life (albeit to the loss of others' lives as well), its egoistic counterpart exhibits a praiseworthy respect and sympathy for the suffering of others (albeit a concern to avoid one's own suffering and sacrifices as well).

Anomic Suicide

Egostic and anomic suicide, as we have seen, are the respective consequences of the individual's insufficient or excessive integration within the society to which he belongs. But quite aside from integrating its members, a society must control and regulate their beliefs and behavior as well; and Durkheim insisted that there is a relation between a society's suicide rate and the way it performs this important regulative function. Industrial and financial crises, for example, increase the suicide rate, a fact commonly attributed to the decline of economic well-being these crises produce. But the same increase in the suicide rate, Durkheim observed, is produced by crisis resulting in economic prosperity; "Every disturbance of equilibrium," he insisted, "even though it achieved greater comfort and a heightening of general vitality, is an impulse to voluntary death" (1897b: 246). But how can this be the case? How can something generally understood to improve a man's life serve to detach him from it?

No living being, Durkheim began, can be happy unless its needs are sufficiently proportioned to its means; for if its needs surpass its capacity to satisfy them, the result can only be friction, pain, lack of productivity, and a general weakening of the impulse to live. In an animal, of course, the desired equilibrium between needs and means is established and maintained by physical nature—the animal cannot imagine ends other than those implicit within its own physiology, and these are ordinarily satisfied by its purely material environment. Human needs, however, are not limited to the body alone; indeed, "beyond the indispensable minimum which satisfies nature when instinctive, a more awakened reflection suggests better conditions, seemingly desirable ends craving fulfillment" (1897b: 247).[13] But the aspirations suggested by such reflections are inherently unlimited; there is nothing in man's individual psychology or physiology which would require them to cease at one point rather than another. Unlimited desires are, by definition, insatiable, and insatiability is a sure source of human misery: "To pursue a goal which is by definition unattainable," Durkheim concluded, "is to condemn oneself to a state of perpetual unhappiness" (1897b: 247–248).

For human beings to be happy, therefore, their individual needs and aspirations must be constrained; and since these needs and aspirations are the products of a reflective social consciousness, the purely internal, physiological constraints enjoyed by animals are insufficient to this purpose. This regulatory function must thus be performed by an external, moral agency superior to the individual—in other words, by society. And since the constraints thus applied are borne unequally by a society's members, the result is a "functional" theory of stratification resembling that of Kingsley Davis and Wilbert Moore[14]—society determines the respective value of different social services, the relative reward allocated to each, and the consequent degree of comfort appropriate to the average worker in each occupation.

This classically conservative doctrine is tempered by two qualifications. First, the scale of services and rewards is not immutable, but rather varies with the amount of collective revenue and the changing moral ideas of the society itself; and second, the system must secure some degree of legitimacy—both the hierarchy of functions and the distribution of these functions among the population must be considered "just" by those subject to it. These caveats entered, however, Durkheim insisted that human happiness can be achieved only through the acceptance of moral (that is, social) constraints.

But what has this to do with suicide? Briefly, when society is disturbed by some crisis, its "scale" is altered and its members are "reclassified"[15] accordingly; in the ensuing period of disequilibrium,

13. This argument—that desires are simple and few in the "state of nature," but multiply with advancing civilization—is one that we (and presumably Durkheim) owe to Rousseau's *Discourse on the Origin of Inequality* (1755).

14. Cf. Davis and Moore, "Some Principles of Stratification", *American Sociological Review*, Vol. X (April, 1945), pp. 242–249.

15. Durkheim used the term "repressive anomy" to describe the condition produced by a reclassification downward in the social hierarchy, and "progressive anomy" to describe its upward counterpart (cf. 1897b: 285).

society is temporarily incapable of exercising its regulative function, and the lack of constraints imposed on human aspirations makes happiness impossible. This explains why periods of economic disaster, like those of sudden prosperity, are accompanied by an increase in the number of suicides, and also why countries long immersed in poverty have enjoyed a relative immunity to self-inflicted death.

Durkheim used the term *anomie* to describe this temporary condition of social deregulation, and *anomic suicide* to describe the resulting type of self-inflicted death; but in one sphere of life, he added, anomie is not a temporary disruption but rather a chronic state. This is the sphere of trade and industry, where the traditional sources of societal regulation—religion, government, and occupational groups—have all failed to exercise moral constraints on an increasingly unregulated capitalist economy. Religion, which once consoled the poor and at least partially restricted the material ambitions of the rich, has simply lost most of its power. Government, which once restrained and subordinated economic functions, is now their servant; thus, the orthodox economist would reduce government to a guarantor of individual contracts, while the extreme socialist would make it the "collective bookkeeper"—and neither would grant it the power to subordinate other social agencies and unite them toward one common aim. Even occupational groups, which once regulated salaries, fixed the price of products and production, and indirectly fixed the average level of income on which needs were based, has been made impotent by the growth of industry and the indefinite expansion of the market. In trade and industry, therefore, "the state of crisis and anomy is constant and, so to speak, normal. From top to bottom of the ladder greed is aroused without knowing where to find ultimate foothold. Nothing can calm it," Durkheim concludes, "since its goal is far beyond all it can attain" (1897b: 256). And thus the industrial and commercial occupations are among those which furnish the greatest numbers of suicides.

Quite aside from such *economic* anomie, however, is that *domestic* anomie which afflicts widows and widowers as well as those who have experienced separation and divorce (cf. Book Two, Chapter 3). The association of the latter with an increased tendency to suicide had already been observed,[16] but had been attributed to marital

---

16. Cf. the study of Bertillon (September, 1882), summarized by Durkheim on p. 260.

selection—divorced couples are more apt to have been recruited from individuals with psychological flaws, who are also more apt to commit suicide. Characteristically, Durkheim rejected such individual, psychological "explanations" for both suicide and divorce, arguing instead that we should focus on the intrinsic nature of marriage and divorce themselves.

Marriage, Durkheim explained, ought to be understood as the social regulation not only of physical instinct, but also of those aesthetic and moral feelings which have become complicated with sexual desire over the course of evolution. Precisely because these new aesthetic and moral inclinations have become increasingly independent of organic necessities, the moral regulation of monogamic marriage has become necessary: "For by forcing a man to attach himself forever to the same woman," Durkheim observed, "it assigns a strictly definite object to the need for love, and closes the horizon" (1897b: 270). Divorce would then be understood as a weakening of this matrimonial regulation, and wherever law and custom permit its "excessive" practice, the relative immunity to self-inflicted death thus guaranteed is undermined, and suicides increase.

As we have already seen, however, the immunity guaranteed by marriage alone is enjoyed only by the husband, both partners participating only in the immunity provided by the larger domestic society; similarly, it is husbands rather than wives who are afflicted with increased suicide rates where divorces are "excessive." Why don't divorce rates affect the wife? Durkheim's quintessentially Victorian answer was that the mental life of women—and thus the "mental character" of their sexual needs—is less developed than that of men; and since their sexual needs are thus more closely related to those of their organism, these needs find an efficient restraint in physiology alone, without the additional, external regulation of that monogamic matrimony required by males. This was an observation, however, from which Durkheim derived an un-Victorian inference: since monogamic matrimony provides no suicidal immunity to the wife, it is a gratuitous form of social discipline which she suffers without the slightest compensatory advantage. The traditional view of marriage—that its purpose is to protect the woman from masculine caprice, and to impose a sacrifice of polygamous instincts upon the man—is thus clearly false; on the contrary, it is the woman who makes the sacrifices, receiving little or nothing in return (1897b: 275–276).

To this "aetiological" classification of suicides by their causes, Durkheim added a "morphological" classification according to their characteristic effects or manifestations. Suicides like that of Lamartine's *Raphael*, for example—committed out of a morbid mood of melancholia—were considered the consequence and expression of *egoistic suicide*, as were the more cheerfully indifferent "Epicurean" suicides of those who, no longer able to experience the pleasures of life, see no reason to prolong it. *Altruistic suicide*, as we have already seen, is characterized by the serene conviction that one is performing one's duty, or a passionate outburst of faith and enthusiasm; while *anomic suicide*, though equally passionate, expresses a mood of anger and disappointment at aspirations unfulfilled.

Just as there are different types of suicide distinguishable by their causes, therefore, there are different species of moods or dispositions through which these types are expressed. In actual experience, however, these types and species are not found in their pure, isolated state; on the contrary, different causes may simultaneously afflict the same individual, giving rise to composite modes of suicidal expression. Egoism and anomie, for example, have a "special affinity" for one another—the socially detached egoist is often unregulated as well (though usually introverted, dispassionate, and lacking in those aspirations which lead to frustration), while the unregulated victim of anomie is frequently a poorly integrated egoist (though his boundless aspirations typically prevent any excessive introversion). Similarly, anomie may be conjoined with altruism—the exasperated infatuation produced by anomie may coincide with the courageous, dutiful resolution of the altruist. Even egoism and altruism, contraries though they are, may combine in certain situations—within a society undergoing disintegration, groups of individuals may construct some ideal out of whole cloth, devoting themselves to it to precisely the extent that they become detached from all else.

Finally, Durkheim found no relation whatsoever between the type of suicide and the nature of the suicidal acts by which death is achieved. Admittedly, there is a correlation between particular societies and the popularity of certain suicidal acts within them, indicating that the choice of suicidal means is determined by social causes. But the causes which lead one to commit suicide in a particular way, Durkheim insisted, are quite different from those which lead one to commit suicide in the first place; the customs and traditions of a particular society place some instruments of death rather than others at one's disposal, and attach differing degrees of dignity even to the various means thus made available. While both are dependent on social causes, therefore, the mode of suicidal act and the nature of suicide itself are unrelated.

SUICIDE AS A SOCIAL PHENOMENON

At any given moment, therefore, the moral constitution of a society—its insufficient or excessive degree of integration or regulation—establishes its contingent rate of voluntary deaths, its "natural aptitude" for suicide; and individual suicidal acts are thus mere extensions and expressions of these underlying currents of egoism, altruism, and anomie. Moreover, the terms that Durkheim employed in making this argument—"collective tendencies," "collective passions," etc.—were not mere metaphors for average individual states; on the contrary, they are "things", *sui generis* forces which dominate the consciousnesses of individuals. In fact, the stability of the suicide rate for any particular society could have no other explanation:

> . . . the numerical equality of annual contingents . . . can only be due to the permanent action of some impersonal cause which transcends all individual cases. . . . The proof that the reality of collective tendencies is no less than that of cosmic forces is that this reality is demonstrated in the same way, by the uniformity of effects. (1897b: 309)[17]

Such an argument, Durkheim admitted, suggests that collective thoughts are of a different nature from individual thoughts, that the former have characteristics which the latter lack. But how can this be, if there are only individuals in society? Durkheim's response was an argument by analogy alluded to in *The Division of Labor* (cf. 1893: 96–100) and developed more fully in "Individual and Collective Representations" (1898). The biological cell, Durkheim observed, is made up exclusively of inanimate atoms; but surely this doesn't mean that there is "nothing more" in animate nature. Similarly, individual human beings, by associating with one another, form a psychical

17. Durkheim thus presented an alternative explanation for a phenomenon—the statistical regularity of certain social phenomena over time—first analyzed scientifically in Adolph Quetelet's *Sur l'homme et le développement de ses facultés ou Essai de physique sociale* (1835) and *Du système social et des lois qui le régissent* (1848). See Durkheim's discussion of these works on pp. 300–304.

existence of a new species, which has its own manner of thinking and feeling: "When the consciousness of individuals, instead of remaining isolated, becomes grouped and combined," Durkheim observed, "something in the world has been altered. Naturally this change produces others, this novelty engenders other novelties, phenomena appear whose characteristic qualities are not found in the elements composing them" (1897b: 310–311). Social life, Durkheim thus admitted, is essentially made up of representations; but collective representations are quite different from their individual counterparts. Indeed, Durkheim had no objection to calling sociology a kind of psychology, so long as we recall that *social* psychology has its own laws which are not those of *individual* psychology.

Moreover, it is simply not true that there are "only individuals" in society. First, a society contains a variety of material things (e.g., written laws, moral precepts and maxims, etc.) which "crystallize" social facts, and act upon the individual from without; and second, beneath these immobilized, sacrosanct forms are the diffused, mingling subjacent sentiments of which these material formulae are the mere signs, and which are equally external to the individual *conscience*. The result was a critique of Quetelet reminiscent of Kant's rejection of any empiricist ethics. Struck by the statistical regularity of certain social phenomena over time, Quetelet had postulated "the average man"—a definite type representing the most generalized characteristics of people in any given society. Such an approach, Durkheim insisted, makes the origin of morality an insoluble mystery; for it conflates the collective type of a society with the average type of its individual members, and since the morality of such individuals reaches only a moderate intensity, the imperative, transcendant character of moral commands is left without an explanation. Beyond the vacuous conception of "God's will," Durkheim insisted, "no alternative exists but to leave morality hanging unexplained in the air or make it a system of collective states of conscience. Morality either springs from nothing given in the world of experience, or it springs from society" (1897b: 318).[18]

In fact, these three currents of opinion—that the individual has a certain personality (egoism), that this personality should be sacrificed if the community required it (altruism), and that the individual is

18. Durkheim insists that the alternative view—that a whole is qualitatively identical with the sum of its parts, and an effect qualitatively reducible to the sum of its causes—would render all change inexplicable; and he again attacks what he takes to be Tarde's defense of this position (cf. 1897b: 311–312).

sensitive to ideas of social progress (anomie)—coexist in all societies, turning individual inclinations in three different and opposed directions. Where these currents offset one another, the individual enjoys a state of equilibrium which protects him from suicide; but where one current exceeds a certain strength relative to others, it becomes a cause of self-inflicted death. Moreover, this strength itself depends on three causes: the nature of the individuals composing the society, the manner of their association, and transitory occurrences which disrupt collective life. The first, of course, is virtually immutable, changing only gradually over a period of centuries; the only variable conditions, therefore, are social conditions, a fact which explains the stability observed by Quetelet so long as society remains unchanged.

The decisive influence of these currents, however, is rarely exerted throughout an entire society; on the contrary, its effect is typically felt within those particular environments whose conditions are especially favorable to the development of one current or another. But the conditions of each individual environment are themselves dependent on the more general conditions of the society as a whole—the force of altruism in the army depends on the role of the military in the larger civilian population; egoistic suicide increases among Protestants to the extent that intellectual individualism is a feature of the entire society; and so on. No collective sentiment can affect individuals, of course, when they are absolutely indisposed to it; but the same social causes that produce these currents also affect the way individuals are socialized, so that a society quite literally produces citizens with the appropriate dispositions at the same time that it molds the currents to which they will thus respond. Durkheim did not deny, therefore, that individual motives have a share in determining who commits suicide; but he did insist that the nature and intensity of the "suicidogenic" current were factors independent of such psychological conditions. Indeed, this was why Durkheim could claim that his theory, however "deterministic," was more consistent with the philosophical doctrine of free will than any psychologistic theory which makes the individual the source of social phenomena; for the intensity of his currents, like the virulence of an infectious disease, determines only the rate at which the population will be affected, not the identity of those to be struck down.

The last remark hinted at what we have seen to be one of Durkheim's preoccupations—his repeated efforts to resolve philosophical quandaries by sociological means; and he soon turned to another: Should suicide be proscribed by morality?[19] This question, Durkheim observed, is typically dealt with by formulating certain general moral principles, and then asking whether suicide logically contradicts these or not. But Durkheim insisted instead on an empirical, sociological approach, examining the way in which real societies have actually treated suicide in the course of history, and then inquiring into the reasons for this treatment. This examination indicated that suicide has been long, widely, and severely condemned, but that such condemnations fell into two categories, indicating two historical stages. In antiquity, suicide was a civil offense, and though the individual was forbidden to end his own life, the state might permit him to do so on certain occasions. But in modern societies, suicide is viewed as a religious crime, and the condemnation is thus both absolute and universal. The distinctive element in the second stage, Durkheim insists, is the Christian conception of the human personality as a "sacred" thing; henceforth, in so far as he retains his identity as a man, the individual shares that quality *sui generis* which religions ascribe to their gods: "He has become tinged with religious value; man has become a god for men. Therefore, any attempt against his life suggests sacrilege" (1897b: 334).

To Montesquieu or to Hume, such an argument, based on a religious premise, was less than compelling. But to Durkheim, agnostic though he was, the religious vestments of the argument were purely symbolic, and did little to discredit it; on the contrary, for Durkheim, every symbol (however mystical) must correspond to something real, and the reality to which the "sacred individual" corresponds is that body of collective sentiments which, with the growth of social volume and density, the division of labor, and individual differences, has elevated the individual personality above that primitive, homogeneous community within which it was literally non-existent.[20] This view that the human person is in some sense

19. See, for example, the famous arguments against such proscription presented in Montesquieu's *Persian Letters* (1721) and Hume's "On Suicide" (1783).

20. This modern "cult of man" should not be confused with the "egoistic individualism" discussed earlier. The latter represents an insufficient state of integration which detaches the individual from society with dangerous consequences; the former unites the members of a society in a single thought, the disinterested impersonal conception of an "ideal humanity" which transcends and subordinates private, selfish goals (cf. 1897b: 336–337).

sacred, Durkheim insisted, is virtually the only common bond joining a modern society's members; far from injuring only himself, therefore, the man who commits suicide violates the most fundamental maxim of the social order, a transgression which is reflected in, and in turn justifies, its severe moral prohibition.

Such an appeal to the sacredness of individual life necessarily raised the question of the relation between suicide and homicide; and this in turn led Durkheim to another attack on the "Italian school" of Ferri and Morselli, for whom such acts were the result of the same psychological cause (moral degeneracy) under different social conditions (suicide is simply a homicide which, repressed by a pacific social environment, is directed back toward the self). Durkheim denied of course that the causes of suicide and homicide are either "psychological" or "the same," and also that the social conditions under which they occur are so consistently different; for, as we have seen, there are different kinds of suicide with different, non-psychological causes, and while some of these are identical to those of homicide, others are quite opposed to them. Egoistic suicide, for example, results from conditions of disintegration and social indifference which, by reducing the intensity of the passions and increasing the respect for the individual, decreases the tendency to homicide. Altruistic suicide, by contrast, springs from a reduced respect for the individual life, as does homicide; but these are the social conditions of primitive rather than civilized societies. Anomic suicide, however, is produced by that more modern mood of exasperation and world-weariness which is equally conducive to homicide; and which kind of death will result is largely determined by the moral constitution of the individual in question. If suicide and homicide vary inversely, Durkheim thus concluded, it is not (*pace* Ferri and Morselli) because they are differing social expressions of the same psychological phenomenon; on the contrary, it is because most modern suicides result from conditions of egoism which are hostile to homicides. And if the relationship between suicide and homicide is not perfectly inverse, it is because the special social conditions which favor either anomic or altruistic suicide are also favorable to homicide.[21]

21. Durkheim recognized that the homicides produced by conditions of anomie and those produced by conditions of altruism could not be "of the same nature"; like suicide, therefore, homicide "is not a single, individual criminological entity, but must include a variety of species very different from one another" (1897b: 358).

Here was another sociological answer to a venerable philosophical question—i.e., whether our feelings for others are mere extensions of our feelings for ourselves or, by contrast, are independent of such selfish sentiments altogether. Durkheim's answer was that both alternatives are misconceived. Feelings for others and feelings for ourselves are not unrelated, but neither does one spring from the other; on the contrary, both are derived from a third source: that estimate of the moral value of the individual rendered by the *conscience collective* at any point in time. Where that estimate is low, as in primitive societies, our indifference to the pain and sadness of others, for example, is matched by our indifference to our own; but where that estimate is high, as in advanced societies, our concern for our own comfort is balanced by a concern for that of others. Our egoistic instincts, of course, will weaken these feelings when applied to the first, and strengthen them in application to the second; but the same moral condition exists and is active in both cases.

Like *The Division of Labor in Society*, *Suicide* concludes with some thoroughly practical questions: What attitude should modern societies take towards suicide? Should reforms be undertaken to restrain it? Or must we accept it as it is? Again as in *The Division of Labor*, Durkheim's answers to these questions depended on whether the current state of suicide is to be considered "normal" or "abnormal"; and, as he had already shown through the example of crime in *The Rules of Sociological Method*, the "immorality" of suicide did not necessarily point to the latter. On the contrary, the statistical data going back to the eighteenth century, as well as legislation surviving from still earlier periods, suggested to Durkheim that suicide was a normal element in the constitution of all societies. In primitive societies and the modern military, for example, the strict subordination of the individual to the group renders altruistic suicide an indispensable part of collective discipline. Again, in societies where the dignity of the person is the supreme end of conduct, egoistic suicide flourishes. And again, in societies where economic progress is rapid and social restraints become slack, anomic suicides are inevitable.

But don't such currents of altruism, egoism, and anomie cause suicide only if excessive? And might such currents not be everywhere maintained at the same level of moderate intensity? Durkheim's initial response echoed his discussion of crime in *The Rules*—there are special environments within each society which can be reached by such currents only if the latter are strengthened or weakened far above or below the more general societal norm. But again, as with crime, these special modifications of the current are not merely necessary; they are also useful, for the most general collective state is simply that best adapted to the most general circumstances, not to those exceptional circumstances to which a society must also be adapted. A society in which intelligent individualism could not be exaggerated, for example, would be incapable of radical innovation, even if such innovation were necessary; inversely, a society in which such individualism could not be significantly reduced would be unable to adapt to the conditions of war, in which conformity and passive obedience are elevated into virtues. It is essential, therefore, that such "special environments" be preserved as a part of the more general existence, so that a society might both respond to particular conditions and evolve gradually over time.[22]

Thus the spirit of renunciation, the taste for individuation, and the love of progress each have their place in every society, and cannot exist without generating suicide. But this does not mean that every suicido-genic current is "normal"; on the contrary, these currents must produce suicides only in a certain measure which varies from one society to another as well as over time. Here Durkheim was particularly concerned to dismiss the view that suicide, the rate of which had increased exponentially in western Europe since the eighteenth century, was the "ransom money" of civilization, the inevitable companion of social progress. The rash of suicides which accompanied the growth of the Roman Empire, Durkheim admitted, might support such a view; but from the height of Rome to the Enlightenment, suicide rates increased only slightly, while Roman culture was assimilated and then surpassed by Christianity, the Renaissance, and the Reformation. Social progress, therefore, does not logically imply suicide, and the undeniably rapid growth of suicide in the late nineteenth century should be attributed not to the intrinsic nature of progress, but rather to these special conditions under which this particular phase of progress has occurred; and even without knowing the nature of these conditions, Durkheim insisted that the very rapidity of this growth indicated that they are morbid

22. Cf. the discussion of crime presented in 1897b: 98–104.

and pathological rather than normal (cf. 1897b: 85–107).[23]

How, then, was this "pathological phenomenon" to be overcome? Durkheim clearly considered the present indulgence toward suicide excessive, but felt that increased penalties for self-inflicted deaths would be inefficacious. The proposed imposition of severe penalties, for example, ignored the fact that suicide is but an exaggeration of acts regarded as virtuous, which a society could hardly be expected resolutely to condemn; and the milder moral penalties (e.g., refusal of burial, denial of civil, political, or familial rights), like education, fail to touch suicide at its source. Indeed, both the legal and the educational systems are themselves products of the same currents that cause suicide itself.

The recent, pathological growth of suicide must thus be attacked at its egoistic and anomic roots.[24] The rapid increase of egoistic suicides, for example, could be attributed to the increasing failure of society to integrate its individual members; and it could be counteracted only by re-establishing the bonds between the individual and the social group: "He must feel himself more solidary with a collective existence which precedes him in time, which survives him, and which encompasses him at all points" (1897b: 373–374).

Which social groups were best prepared to exercise this reintegrative function? Certainly not the state, Durkheim insisted, for political society is too distant from the individual to affect his life forcefully and continuously. Neither is religion a binding force; for while the Roman Catholic Church once exercised an integrative influence, it did so at the cost of a freedom of thought it no longer has the authority to command. Even the family, traditionally the central cohesive force in the life of the individual, has proved susceptible to the same disintegrative currents responsible for the rapid increase of suicide. In fact, the state, religion, and the family were able to prevent suicides only because they were cohesive, integrated societies in themselves; and, having lost that character, they no longer have that effect.

23. To these symptoms of pathology Durkheim adds the rise of philosophical pessimism. Comparing his own intellectual milieu with that of Zeno and Epicurus, he points to the systems of Schopenhauer and Hartmann, and the more broadly based intellectual movements of anarchism, aestheticism, mysticism, and revolutionary socialism as evidence of a "collective melancholy" which "would not have penetrated consciousness so far if it had not undergone a morbid development" (1897b: 370).

24. The causes of altruistic suicide, as we have seen, played no role in the "morbid effervescence" of nineteenth-century suicides, and appeared instead to be declining. Fatalistic suicide was already a subject of merely historical interest.

But there is a group—the "occupational group" or "corporation"—that has enormous integrative and thus preventative potential. "Its influence on individuals is not intermittent," Durkheim emphasized, for "it is always in contact with them by the constant exercise of the function of which it is the organ and in which they collaborate. It follows the workers wherever they go. . . . Wherever they are, they find it enveloping them, recalling them to their duties, supporting them at need. Finally," he concluded, "corporate action makes itself felt in every detail of our occupations, which are thus given a collective orientation" (1897b: 379).[25]

To fulfill this potential, however, the occupational groups must become a recognized organ of public life, outside of (though subject to)[26] the state, and be granted definite social functions—the supervision of insurance, welfare, and pensions; the settling of contractual disputes; the regulation of working conditions; etc. But above all, the occupational group must exercise a *moral* function: "Besides the rights and duties common to all men," Durkheim explained, "there are others depending on qualities peculiar to each occupation, the number of which increases in importance as occupational activity increasingly develops and diversifies. For each of these special disciplines," he concluded, "an equally special organ is needed, to apply and maintain it" (1897b: 380).

But if this is the best way to combat "corrosive individual egoism," it is also the best means to combat anomie;[27] for the same groups that

25. Cf. the important Preface to the second edition of *The Division of Labor* (1902), which extends this argument.

26. The failure of the state to perform this regulative function in the past, Durkheim suggests, led to the eventual suppression of the medieval guilds altogether: ". . . if similar corporations of different localities had been connected with one another, instead of remaining isolated, so as to form a single system, if all these systems had been subject to the general influence of the State and thus kept in constant awareness of their solidarity, bureaucratic despotism and occupational egoism would have been kept within proper limits" (1897b: 381–382).

27. Though not all kinds of anomie. The only way to reduce suicides arising from *conjugal anomie* (i.e., divorce), Durkheim suggests, is to make marriage more indissoluble; but by thus diminishing the suicides of husbands, we would also increase those of wives, for whom the matrimonial bond is of considerably less benefit. This dilemma can be overcome, however, if we recall that the differential advantage enjoyed by the husband is due to the fact that his aspirations are of societal origin, while the wife is more influenced by physiology. While Durkheim was sure that a woman could never fulfill the same social functions as a man, therefore, he still felt that granting women a more active and important role in society would eventually secure them the same advantages from matrimony hitherto enjoyed only by men (cf. 1897b: 384–386).

re-integrate the individual into social life can also serve to regulate his aspirations: "Whenever excited appetites tended to exceed all limits," Durkheim explained,

> the corporation would have to decide the share that should equitably revert to each of the cooperative parts. Standing above its own members, it would have all necessary authority to demand indispensable sacrifices and concessions and impose order upon them. . . . Thus, a new sort of moral discipline would be established, without which all the scientific discoveries and economic progress in the world could produce only malcontents. (1897b: 383)[28]

The pathological increase in suicides is thus a result of the "moral poverty" of our age, Durkheim insisted, and a new moral discipline is required to cure it; but as always, he insisted that this moral poverty itself had structural causes, and thus a reform of social structure (i.e., decentralized occupational groups)[29] was required to relieve its most morbid symptoms.

CRITICAL REMARKS

As the first systematic application of the methodological principles set out in his "manifesto" of 1895, *Suicide* reveals their limitations as well as their advantages, and thus provides an occasion for considering a number of difficulties—argument by elimination, *petitio principii*, an inappropriate and distortive language, etc.— which, though typical of Durkheim's work as a whole, are perhaps

28. This parallel efficacy is due to the fact that, at least in part, anomie results from the same *cause*—the "disaggregation" of social forces—as does egoism; but in each case, the *effect* is different, depending on the "point of incidence" of this cause, and whether it "influences active and practical functions, or functions that are representative. The former it agitates and exasperates; the latter it disorients and disconcerts" (1897b: 382).

29. "Decentralization" was the watchword of a number of Durkheim's contemporaries who, recognizing the impotence of the monolithic state in the face of egoism and anomie, sought to restore to local groups some of their old autonomy. Durkheim's proposed reform was thus a specific variation on this more general theme. The particular advantage of *occupational* decentralization, he urged, is that, because each of these new centers of moral life would be the focus of only specialized activity, the individual could become attached to them, and they could become attached to one another, without the solidarity of the country as a whole being undermined (cf. 1897b: 390–391).

most clearly seen here. Durkheim's characteristic "argument by elimination," for example, pervades both *The Division of Labor* and *The Elementary Forms*, but there is no better example of its power to both persuade and mislead than Durkheim's discussion of "extra-social causes" in Book One of *Suicide*. Briefly, the argument consists of the systematic rejection of alternative definitions or explanations of a social fact, in a manner clearly intended to lend credibility to the sole remaining candidate—which is Durkheim's own. Durkheim's use of this technique, of course, does not imply that his candidate does not deserve to be elected; but as a rhetorical device, argument by elimination runs at least two serious risks: first, that the alternative definitions and/or explanations might not be jointly exhaustive (other alternatives may exist); and, more seriously, that the alternative definitions and/or explanations might not be mutually exclusive (the conditions and causes they postulate separately might be conjoined to form perfectly adequate definitions and/or explanations other than Durkheim's "sole remaining" candidates). Durkheim's persistent use of this strategy can be attributed to his ineradicable belief, clearly stated in *The Rules*, that a given effect must always have a single cause, and that this cause must be of the same nature as the effect (Lukes, 1972: 31–33).

Petitio principii—the logical fallacy in which the premise of an argument *presumes* the very conclusion yet to be argued—is, again, a feature of Durkheim's work as a whole. In *The Elementary Forms*, for example, Durkheim first defined religion as a body of beliefs and practices uniting followers in a single community, and later he concluded that this is one of religion's major functions. But there is no clearer instance of this style of argument than Durkheim's "aetiological" classification of the types of suicide, which of course presupposes the validity of the causal explanations eventually proposed for them. The point, again, is not that this automatically destroys Durkheim's argument; but it does make it impossible to entertain alternative causes and typologies, and thus to evaluate Durkheim's frequently ambitious claims (cf. Lukes, 1972: 31).

Durkheim's repeated insistence that sociology is a science with its own, irreducible "reality" to study also led him to adopt a language that was both highly metaphorical and systematically misleading. This is first evident in *The Division of Labor*, where abundant biological metaphors continuously suggest that society is "like" an organism in a variety of unspecified and unqualified ways; and it is still more pernicious in *The Elementary Forms*, where the real themes of the work—the social origin of religious beliefs and rituals, their symbolic meanings, etc.—are frequently disguised beneath the obfuscatory language of "electrical currents" and "physical forces."[30] *Suicide* combines the worst elements of both; and in particular, this language made it difficult if not impossible for Durkheim to speak intelligibly about the way in which individual human beings perceive, interpret, and respond to "suicido-genic" social conditions (cf. Lukes, 1972: 34–36).

Finally, it might be argued that Durkheim's central explanatory hypothesis—that, when social conditions fail to provide people with the necessary social goals and/or rules at the appropriate levels of intensity, their socio-psychological health is impaired, and the most vulnerable among them commit suicide—raises far more questions than it answers. Aren't there different kinds of "social goals and rules," for example, and aren't some of these *dis*-harmonious? What *is* socio-psychological "health"? Isn't it socially determined, and thus relative to the particular society or historical period in question? Why are disintegrative, egoistic appetites always described as individual, psychological, and even organic in origin? Aren't some of our most disruptive drives socially generated? And if they are, aren't they also culturally relative? Why are some individuals rather than others "impaired"? And what is the relationship (if, indeed, there is one) between such impairment and suicide? The fact that these questions and others are continuously begged simply reiterates an earlier point—that Durkheim's macro-sociological explanations all presuppose some social-psychological theory, whose precise nature is never made explicit (cf. Lukes, 1972: 213–222).

---

30. In his defense of *The Elementary Forms* before the Société française de philosophie (1913). Durkheim insisted that his primary concern had been to point out the "dynamo-genic" quality of religious belief.

Reason, Religion, and Society: The Elementary Forms of the Religious Life (1912)

DURKHEIM'S TWO PROBLEMS

Durkheim's primary purpose in *The Elementary Forms* was to describe and explain the most primitive[1] religion known to man. But if his interests thus bore some external similarity to those of the ethnographer or historian, his ultimate purpose went well beyond the reconstruction of an archaic culture for its own sake; on the contrary, as in *The Division of Labor* and *Suicide*, Durkheim's concern was ultimately both present and practical: "If we have taken primitive religion as the subject of our research," he insisted, "it is because it has seemed to us better adapted than any other to lead to an understanding of the religious nature of man, that is to say, to show us an essential and permanent aspect of humanity" (1912: 13).

But if Durkheim's goal was thus to understand modern man, why did he go to the very beginning of history? How can the crude cults of the Australian aborigines tell us anything about religions far more advanced in value, dignity, and truth? And if he insisted that they can, wasn't he suggesting that Christianity, for example, proceeds from the same primitive mentality as the Australian cults? These questions were important, for Durkheim recognized that scholars

1. A religious system may be said to be "most primitive" when: (a) it is found in a society whose organization is surpassed by no others in simplicity; and (b) it is possible to explain this system without using any element borrowed from any previous religion (cf. 1912: 13).

frequently focused on primitive religions in order to discredit their modern counterparts, and he rejected this "Voltairean" hostility to religion for two reasons. First, alluding to the second chapter of *The Rules*, Durkheim insisted that such hostility was unscientific; it prejudges the results of the investigation, and renders its outcome suspect. Second, and more important, he considered it unsociological; for it is an essential postulate of sociology that no human institution can rest on an error or a lie. If an institution is not based on "the nature of things," Durkheim insisted, it encounters a resistance in nature which destroys it; the very existence of primitive religions, therefore, assures us that they "hold to reality and express it." The symbols through which this reality is expressed, of course, may seem absurd; but we must know how to go beneath the symbol, to uncover the reality which it represents, and which gives it its meaning: "The most barbarous and the most fantastic rites and the strangest myths translate some human need, some aspect of life, either individual or social. The reasons with which the faithful justify them may be, and generally are, erroneous; but the true reasons," Durkheim concluded, "do not cease to exist, and it is the duty of science to discover them" (1912: 14–15).

In this sense, *all* religions are "true"; but if all religions are thus equal with respect to the reality they express, why did Durkheim focus on *primitive* religions in particular? Briefly, he did so for three "methodological" reasons. First, Durkheim argued that we cannot understand more advanced religions except by analyzing the way they have been progressively constituted throughout history; for only by placing each of the constituent elements of modern religions in the context within which it emerged can we hope to discover the cause which gave rise to it.[2] In this analysis, as in Cartesian logic, the first link of the chain was the most important; but for Durkheim, this link at the foundation of the science of religions was not a "conceptual possibility" but a concrete reality based on historical and ethnographic observations. Just as biological evolution has been differently conceived since the empirical discovery of monocellular beings, therefore, religious evolution is differently conceived depending upon what concrete system of belief and action is placed at its origin.

Second, Durkheim suggested that the scientific study of religion itself presupposed that the various religions we compare are all

2. Cf. Durkheim's "Rules for the Demonstration of Sociological Proof" (1895: 145–158).

species of the same class, and thus possess certain elements in common: "At the foundation of all systems of belief and all cults," Durkheim thus argued,

> there ought necessarily to be a certain number of fundamental representations or conceptions and of ritual attitudes which, in spite of the diversity of forms which they have taken, have the same objective significance and fulfill the same functions everywhere. These are the permanent elements which constitute that which is permanent and human in religion; they form all the objective contents of the idea which is expressed when one speaks of *religion* in general. (1912: 17)

Again, therefore, Durkheim was trying to answer a time-honored philosophical question (the "essential nature" of religion) by new, sociological means (the ethnography of primitive societies); and the special value of such ethnographies was that they captured religious ideas and practices before priests, prophets, theologians, or the popular imagination had had the opportunity to refine and transform them:

> That which is accessory or secondary . . . has not yet come to hide the principal elements. All is reduced to that which is indispensable, to that without which there could be no religion. But that which is indispensable is also that which is essential, that is to say, that which we must know before all else. (1912: 18)

Primitive religions are *privileged* cases, Durkheim thus argued, because they are *simple* cases.

But if this simplicity of primitive religions helps us to understand its nature, it also helps us to understand its causes. In fact, as religious thought evolved through history, its initial causes became overlaid with a vast scheme of methodological and theological interpretation which made those origins virtually imperceptible. The study of primitive religion, Durkheim thus suggested, is a new way of taking up the old problem of the "origin of religion" itself—not in the sense of some specific point in time and space when religion began to exist (no such point exists), but in the sense of discovering "the ever-present causes upon which the most essential forms of religious thought and practice depend" (1912: 20).

This description and explanation of the most primitive religion, however, was only the primary purpose of *The Elementary Forms*;

and its secondary purpose was by far the most ambitious of Durkheim's attempts to provide sociological answers to philosophical questions. At the base of all our judgments, Durkheim began, there are a certain number of ideas which philosophers since Aristotle have called "the categories of the understanding"—time, space, class, number, cause, substance, personality, and so on.[3] Such ideas "correspond to the most universal properties of things. They are like the solid frame which encloses all thought; this does not seem to be able to liberate itself from them without destroying itself, for it seems that we cannot think of objects that are not in time and space, which have no number, etc." (1912: 22).

How are these ideas related to religion? When primitive religious beliefs are analyzed, Durkheim observed, these "categories" are found, suggesting that they are the product of religious thought; but religious thought itself is composed of collective representations, the products of real social groups. These observations suggested to Durkheim that the "problem of knowledge" might be posed in new, sociological terms. Previous efforts to solve this problem, he began, represent one of two philosophical doctrines: the *empiricist* doctrine that the categories are constructed out of human experience, and that the individual is the artisan of this construction, and the *a priorist* doctrine that the categories are logically prior to experience, and are inherent in the nature of the human intellect itself. The difficulty for the *empirical* thesis, Durkheim then observed, is that it deprives the categories of their most distinctive properties—universality (they are the most general concepts we have, are applicable to all that is real, and are independent of every particular object) and necessity (we literally cannot think without them); for it is in the very nature of empirical data that they be both particular and contingent. The *a priorist* thesis, by contrast, has more respect for these properties of universality and necessity; but by asserting that the categories simply "inhere" in the nature of the intellect, it begs what is surely the most interesting and important question of all: "It is necessary," Durkheim insisted, "to show whence we hold this surprising prerogative and

3. Although Durkheim's arguments here reveal his enormous debt to Kant and the French neo-Kantian Charles Renouvier (1815–1903), his more specific source was Renouvier's follower Octave Hamelin (1856–1907). Where Kant had described time and space as "forms of intuition" rather than among the twelve categories of the understanding, for example, Durkheim's decision to treat them as categories reflects the influence of Hamelin's *Essai sur les éléments principaux de la représentation* (1907) (cf. Durkheim, 1912: 21 n. 4).

how it comes that we can see certain relations in things which the examination of these things cannot reveal to us" (1912: 27). In sum, if reason is simply a variety of individual experience, it no longer exists; but if its distinctive properties are recognized but not explained, it is set beyond the bounds of nature and thus of scientific investigation. Having planted these (allegedly) formidable obstacles in the paths of his philosophical adversaries, Durkheim then offered his frustrated reader an attractive *via media*: " . . . if the social origin of the categories is admitted," he suggested, "a new attitude becomes possible which we believe will enable us to escape both of the opposed difficulties" (1912: 28).

How, then, does the hypothesis of the social origin of the categories overcome these obstacles? First, the basic proposition of the *a priorist* thesis is that knowledge is composed of two elements—perceptions mediated by our senses, and the categories of the understanding—neither of which can be reduced to the other. By viewing the first as individual representations and the second as their collective counterparts, Durkheim insisted, this proposition is left intact; for "between these two sorts of representations there is all the difference which exists between the individual and the social, and one can no more derive the second from the first than he can deduce society from the individual, the whole from the part, the complex from the simple" (1912: 28). Second, this hypothesis is equally consistent with the duality of human nature—just as our moral ideals are irreducible to our utilitarian motives, so our reason is irreducible to our experience. In so far as we belong to society, therefore, we transcend our individual nature both when we act and when we think. Finally, this distinction explains both the universality and the necessity of the categories—they are universal because man has always and everywhere lived in society, which is their origin; and they are necessary because, without them, all contact between individual minds would be impossible, and social life would be destroyed altogether: " . . . society could not abandon the categories to the free choice of the individual without abandoning itself. If it is to live," Durkheim concluded, "there is not merely need of a satisfactory moral conformity, but also there is a minimum of logical conformity beyond which it cannot safely go" (1912: 30).[4]

4. Durkheim suggested that this explains the exceptional authority inherent in our reason—it is simply the authority of society, transferred to that part of our thought which is the indispensable foundation of all common action.

But one might still object that, since the categories are mere representations of *social* realities, there is no guarantee of their correspondence to any of the realities of *nature*; thus we would return, by a different route, to a more skeptical nominalism and empiricism.[5] Durkheim's rationalist and rather metaphysical answer is that society itself is a part of nature, and "it is impossible that nature should differ radically from itself . . . in regard to that which is most essential. The fundamental relations between things—just that which it is the function of the categories to express—cannot be essentially dissimilar in the different realms" (1912: 31).

DEFINING RELIGION

In order to describe and explain the most primitive religion known to man, Durkheim observed, we must first define the term "religion" itself; otherwise we risk drawing inferences from beliefs and practices which have nothing "religious" about them, or (and this was the greater danger to Durkheim) of leaving many religious facts to one side without understanding their true nature.[6] In fact, Durkheim had already made such an attempt in "Concerning the Definition of Religious Phenomena" (1899), where he argued that religion consists of "obligatory beliefs united with definite practices which relate to the objects given in the beliefs" (1899: 93). While this definition achieved a number of aims, however (cf. Lukes, 1972: 241–243), Durkheim soon became displeased with its overriding emphasis on "obligation"; and, as he later acknowledged (cf. 1912: 37 n. 1, 63 n. 68), the definition offered in 1912 is significantly different.[7]

Following *The Rules* (1895: 72–75) and *Suicide* (1897: 42–46), Durkheim's 1912 definition is reached by a two-step process. First, he insisted, we must free the mind of all preconceived ideas of religion, a liberation achieved in *The Elementary Forms* through a characteristic

5. More strongly, Lukes (1972: 437) suggests that this implies a conventionalism and extreme relativism.

6. This second remark is particularly directed at James Frazer, whose essay, "The Origin of Totemism" (1899) had argued that the beliefs and practices of the Australian aborigines, also the focus of *The Elementary Forms*, were largely magical rather than religious in nature.

7. In a recent essay (Jones, 1985), I have tried to explain the reasons for this displeasure, placing particular emphasis on the ethnographic data presented in Spencer and Gillen's *Native Tribes in Central Australia* (1899), and especially its Frazerian interpretation (1899).

"argument by elimination": "it is fitting," Durkheim suggested, "to examine some of the most current of the definitions in which these prejudices are commonly expressed, before taking up the question on our own account" (1912: 39). Second, Durkheim proposed to examine the various religious systems we know in their concrete reality, in order to determine those elements which they have in common; for "religion cannot be defined except by the characteristics which are found wherever religion itself is found" (1912: 38).

The first of the prejudicial definitions of religion to be eliminated by this procedure was that governed by our ideas of those things which surpass the limits of our knowledge—the "mysterious," the "unknowable," the "supernatural"—whereby religion would be "a sort of speculation upon all that which evades science or distinct thought in general" (1912: 39).[8] Durkheim saw at least four discernible difficulties in such a definition. First, while he admitted that the sense of mystery has played a considerable role in the history of some religions, and especially Christianity, he added that, even in Christianity, there have been periods—e.g., the scholastic period (tenth to fifteenth centuries), the seventeeth century, etc.—in which this sense was virtually non-existent. Second, while Durkheim agreed that the forces put in operation by some primitive rite designed to assure the fertility of the soil or the fecundity of an animal species appear "different" from those of modern science, he denied that this distinction between religious and physical forces is perceived by those performing the rite; the abyss which separates the rational from the irrational, Durkheim emphasized, belongs to a much later period in history. Third, and more specifically, the very idea of the "supernatural" logically presupposes its contrary—the idea of a "natural order of things" or "natural law"—to which the supernatural event or entity is presumably a dramatic exception; but the idea of natural law, Durkheim again suggested, is a still more recent conception than that of the distinction between religious and physical forces.[9] Finally,

8. Among the works in which such a definition is entertained, Durkheim suggests, are Herbert Spencer's *First Principles* (1862) and F. Max Müller's *Introduction to the Science of Religion* (1873) and *Lectures on the Origin and Growth of Religion* (1878).

9. This observation provides Durkheim with the opportunity for some caustic remarks on that intellectual field from which such "primitive" thinking has not yet disappeared—the social sciences: "There are only a small number of minds," he suggests, "which are strongly penetrated with this idea that societies are subject to natural laws and form a kingdom of nature. It follows that veritable miracles are believed to be possible there" (1912: 41).

Durkheim simply denied that the object of religious conceptions is that which is "exceptional" or "abnormal"; on the contrary, the gods frequently serve to account for that which is constant and ordinary— "for the regular march of the universe, for the movement of the stars, the rhythm of the seasons, the annual growth of vegetation, the perpetuation of species, etc. It is far from being true," Durkheim concluded, "that the notion of the religious coincides with that of the extraordinary or the unforeseen" (1912: 43).

The second prejudicial definition rejected by Durkheim was that based upon the idea of "gods"[10] or, more broadly, "spiritual beings."[11] The relations we can have with such beings, Durkheim observed, are determined by the nature attributed to them—they are *conscious* beings, and thus we can act upon them only through *conscious* processes (invocations, prayers, offerings, sacrifices); and since the object of religion is to govern our relations with such beings, there can be no religion except where such conscious processes are at work. The difficulty for this definition, Durkheim insisted, is that it fails to acknowledge two categories of undeniably religious facts. First, there are great religions (e.g., Buddhism, Jainism, Brahminism, etc.) from which the idea of gods or spirits is almost absent, and in which the "conscious processes" indicated above play a minor role at best. Second, even within those religions which do acknowledge such beings, there are many rites which are completely independent of that idea, and in some cases the idea is itself derived from the rite rather than the reverse.[12] "All religious powers," Durkheim concludes, "do not emanate from divine personalities, and there are relations of cult which have other objects when uniting man to a deity. Religion is more than the idea of gods or spirits, and consequently cannot be defined exclusively in relation to these latter" (1912: 50).

Definition by the ideas of "spiritual beings" and "the supernatural" thus eliminated, Durkheim turned to the construction of his own definition. Emphasizing that religion is less an indivisible whole than a complex system of parts, he began by dividing these parts into *rites* (determined modes of action) and *beliefs* (collective representations);

10. Cf. Albert Réville's *Prolégomènes de l'histoire des religions* (1881).

11. Cf. E.B. Tylor's *Primitive Culture* (1871).

12. The "ritual theory of myth" advanced by Robertson Smith (1889: 18–22) suggested that the earliest religions consisted primarily of actions rather than ideas, and that the latter were adopted as *ex post facto* rationalizations of the former.

and since rites can be distinguished from other actions only by their object, and the nature of that object is determined by the beliefs, Durkheim insisted on defining the latter first. "All known religious beliefs," he observed, "present one common characteristic: they presuppose a classification of all the things, real and ideal, of which men think, into two classes or opposed groups, generally designated by two distinct terms which are translated well enough by the words *profane* and *sacred*" (1912: 52). The characteristic by which the latter is distinguished from the former, moreover, is simply that it is distinguished *absolutely*:[13] "In all the history of human thought," Durkheim emphasized, "there exists no other example of two categories of things so profoundly differentiated or so radically opposed to one another" (1912: 53).[14] Durkheim thus arrived at his preliminary definition of the essential parts of any religious system: *sacred things* are those isolated and protected by powerful interdictions; *profane things* are those which, according to those interdictions, must remain at a distance from their sacred counterparts; *religious beliefs* are representations which express the nature of sacred things and their relations, either with one another or with profane things; *religious rites* are rules of conduct which prescribe how one should behave in the presence of sacred things; and finally, where "a certain number of sacred things sustain relations of co-ordination or subordination with each other in such a way as to form a system having a certain unity," the beliefs and rites thus united constitute a *religion* (1912: 56).

The seemingly insuperable obstacle to the immediate acceptance of this definition was its subsumption of a body of facts ordinarily distinguished from religion—i.e., *magic*. Indeed, magic is also composed of beliefs and rites, myths, dogmas, sacrifices, lustrations,

13. Durkheim considered the suggestion that sacred things are superior to profane things, either in dignity or in power, but concluded that: (a) there is nothing inherently "religious" in most distinctions between superior and inferior; (b) many sacred things have little dignity or power; and (c) even where men are dependent upon, and thus in some sense inferior to, their gods, the gods are also dependent upon their worshippers. The relationship is reciprocal (cf. 1912: 52–53).

14. Such emphasis is not without qualifications. *Within* the two classes, for example, there are "secondary species" equally opposed to one another (cf. 1912: 434–461 and below); and even *between* the two classes, the separation must be such as to permit some degree of communication of the sacred with the profane. Such communication requires elaborate ritual precautions, however, and even so, the two classes "cannot ... approach each other and keep their own nature at the same time" (1912: 55).

prayers, chants, and dances as well; and the beings and forces invoked by the magician are not only similar to those addressed by religion, but are frequently the same. Yet historically, magic and religion have frequently exhibited a marked repugnance for one another,[15] suggesting that any definition of the latter should find some means of excluding the former. For Durkheim, this means was Robertson Smith's insistence, in his *Lectures on the Religion of the Semites* (1889: 90, 264–265), that religion was a public, social, beneficent institution, while magic was private, selfish, and at least potentially maleficent. "The really religious beliefs," Durkheim could thus argue, "are always common to a determined group or 'Church,' which makes a profession of adhering to them and of practicing the rites connected with them. . . . The individuals which compose it feel themselves united to each other by the simple fact that they have a common faith" (1912: 59).[16] The belief in magic, by contrast,

> does not result in binding together those who adhere to it, nor in uniting them into a group leading a common life. . . . Between the magician and the individuals who consult him, as between these individuals themselves, there are no lasting bonds which make them members of the same moral community, comparable to that formed by the believers in the same god or the observers of the same cult. (1912: 60)[17]

Hence Durkheim's definition: "*A religion is a unified system of beliefs and practices relative to sacred things, that is to say, things set apart and forbidden—beliefs and practices which unite into one single moral community called a Church, all those who adhere to them*" (1912: 62).

15. Here Durkheim profited from Hubert and Mauss's "Esquisse d'un théorie génerale de la magie" (1904).

16. This criterion itself faced difficulties in the so-called "private religions" which individuals establish and celebrate by themselves; but, while acknowledging the recent and increasing popularity of these "individual cults," Durkheim insisted that they "are not distinct and autonomous religious systems, but merely aspects of the common religion of the whole Church, of which the individuals are members. . . ." (1912: 61).

17. Here again, Durkheim faced difficulties in the so-called "societies of magicians"; but such societies, he responded, are not essential to the efficacy of the magical rite itself, nor do they include the "layman" for whom such rites are celebrated (1912: 60–61).

THE MOST PRIMITIVE RELIGION

Armed with his "preliminary definition" of religion, Durkheim set out in search of its most primitive, elementary form. Almost immediately, however, another difficulty arose—even the crudest religions of which we have any historical or ethnographic knowledge appear to be the products of a long, rather complicated evolution, and thus exhibit a profusion of beliefs and rites based upon a variety of "essential" principles. To discover the "truly original" form of the religious life, Durkheim observed, it is thus necessary "to descend by analysis beyond these observable religions, to resolve them into their common and fundamental elements, and then to seek among these latter some one from which the others were derived" (1912: 64). The problem, in short, was less one of describing and explaining a system of observable beliefs and practices than of constructing the hypothetical, essential origin from which these later religions presumably derived.

This was a problem for which two contrary solutions had been proposed, based upon the two common elements found universally among the observable religions. One set of beliefs and practices, for example, is addressed to the phenomena of nature, and is thus characterized as *naturism*; while a second body of religious thought and action appeals to conscious spiritual beings, and is called *animism*. The problem of accounting for the confusing properties of the observable religions thus resolved itself into two mutually contradictory evolutionary hypotheses: either animism was the most primitive religion, and naturism its secondary, derivative form; or the cult of nature stood at the origin of religion, and the cult of spirits was but a peculiar, subsequent development.[18] It was through the critical examination of these traditional theories—another argument by elimination—that Durkheim hoped to reveal the need for a new theory altogether.

18. Neither the problem nor Durkheim's account of it was quite so simple. First, Durkheim at least temporarily ignored all theories which appealed to "super-experimental" data—e.g., Andrew Lang's appeal, in *The Making of Religion* (1898), to a direct intuition of the divine, or the similar view of Wilhelm Schmidt developed in "L'Origine de l'idée de Dieu" (1908–1910)—though he took these up later (cf. 1912: 322–332). Second, Durkheim admitted the possibility of combining the two theories—as Fustel de Coulanges had done in *La Cité antique* (1864)—in which case we must decide what place to grant each. And third, Durkheim also acknowledged the efforts of some scholars to use certain propositions in these theories without adopting either in its systematic form (cf. 1912: 65).

Animism

According to the animistic theory, the idea of the human soul was first suggested by the contrast between the mental representations experienced while asleep (dreams) and those of normal experience. The primitive man grants equal status to both, and is thus led to postulate a "second self" within him, one resembling the first, but made of an ethereal matter and capable of traveling great distances in short periods of time. The transformation of this soul into a spirit is achieved with death, which, to the primitive mind, is not unlike a prolonged sleep; and with the destruction of the body comes the idea of spirits detached from any organism and wandering about freely in space. Henceforth, spirits are assumed to involve themselves, for good or ill, in the affairs of men, and all human events varying slightly from the ordinary are attributed to their influence. As their power grows, men increasingly consider it wise to conciliate their favor or appease them when they are irritated, whence come prayers, offerings, sacrifices—in short, the entire apparatus of religious worship. Reasoning wholly by analogy, the primitive mind also attributes a "second self" to all non-human objects—plants, animals, rivers, trees, stars, etc.—which thus accounts for the phenomena of the physical world; and thus, the ancestor cult gives rise to the cult of nature. In the end, Durkheim concluded, "men find themselves the prisoners of this imaginary world of which they are, however, the authors and models" (1912: 68).[19]

If this animistic hypothesis is to be accepted as an account of the most primitive religion, Durkheim observed, three parts of the argument are of critical significance: its demonstration that the idea of the soul was formed without borrowing elements from any prior religion; its account of how souls become spirits, and thus the objects

19. Durkheim's summary of the animistic hypothesis constructed from Tylor's *Primitive Culture* (1871) and Spencer's *Principles of Sociology*, Parts I (1876) and VI (1885). The two treatments are largely similar, although Spencer rejects Tylor's appeal to primitive analogical reasoning as an explanation of the cult of nature; the belief that non-human objects have souls, Spencer argued, was rather the result of metaphorical names (e.g., of a plant, animal, star, etc.) being given to children at birth, but later taken as literal in a "confusion of language," so that the non-human object was assumed to be the child's ancestor, and becomes the object of worship. Durkheim rejects Spencer's explanation, however, arguing that errors of language are insufficiently general to account for an institution of the universality of the cult of nature (cf. 1912: 70–71).

of a cult; and its derivation of the cult of nature from ancestor worship. Doubts concerning the first were already raised by the observation, to be discussed later (cf. 1912: 273–308), that the soul, though independent of the body under certain conditions, is in fact considerably more intimately bound to the organism than the animistic hypothesis would suggest. Even if these doubts were overcome, moreover, the animistic theory presumes that dreams are liable to but one primitive interpretation—that of a "second-self"— when the interpretive possibilities are in fact innumerable; and even were this objection removed, defenders of the hypothesis must still explain why primitive men, otherwise so unreflective, were presumably driven to "explain" their dreams in the first place.

The "very heart of the animist doctrine," however, was its second part—the explanation of how souls become spirits and objects of a cult; but here again Durkheim had serious doubts. Even if the analogy between sleep and death were sufficient to suggest that the soul survives the body, for example, this still fails to explain why the soul would thus become a "sacred" spirit, particularly in light of the tremendous gap which separates the sacred from the profane, and the fact that the approach of death is ordinarily assumed to weaken rather than strengthen the vital energies of the soul. Most important, however, if the first sacred spirits were souls of the dead, then the lower the society under investigation, the greater should be the place given to the ancestor cult; but, on the contrary, the ancestor cult is clearly developed only in relatively advanced societies (e.g., China, Egypt, Greece and Rome) while it is completely lacking among the most primitive Australian tribes.

But even if ancestor worship *were* primitive, Durkheim continued, the third part of the animist theory—the transformation of the ancestor cult into the cult of nature—is indefensible in itself. Not only is there little evidence among primitives of the complicated analogical reasoning upon which the animist hypothesis depends; neither is there evidence among those practicing any form of nature worship of those characteristics—anthropomorphic spirits, or spirits exhibiting at least some of the attributes of a human soul—which their derivation from the ancestor cult would logically suggest.

For Durkheim, however, the clearest refutation of the animistic hypothesis lay in one of its unstated, but implied, consequences; for, if it were true, not only would it mean (as Durkheim himself believed) that religious symbols provide only an inexact expression of the realities on which they are based; far more than this, it would imply that religious symbols are products of the vague, ill-conceived hallucinations of our dream-experience, and thus (as Durkheim most certainly did *not* believe) have no foundation in reality at all. Law, morals, even scientific thought itself, Durkheim observed, were born of religion, long remained confounded with it, and are still somewhat imbued with its spirit; it is simply inconceivable, therefore, that "religions, which have held so considerable a place in history, and to **which, in all times, men have to receive the energy which they must have to live, should be made up of a tissue of illusions"** (1912: 87). Indeed, the animistic hypothesis is inconsistent with the scientific study of religion itself; for a science is always a discipline applied to the study of some real phenomenon of nature, while animism reduces religion to a mere hallucination. What sort of science is it, Durkheim asked, whose principle discovery is that the subject of which it treats does not exist?

Naturism

In sharp contrast to animism, the naturistic theory[20] insisted that religion ultimately rests upon a real experience—that of the principal phenomena of nature (the infinity of time, space, force, etc.)—which is sufficient to directly arouse religious ideas in the mind. But religion itself begins only when these natural forces cease being represented in the mind in an abstract form, and are transformed into personal, conscious spirits or gods, to whom the cult of nature may be addressed; and this transformation is (allegedly) achieved by language. Before the ancient Indo-European peoples began to reflect upon and classify the phenomena of nature, Durkheim explained, the roots of their language consisted of very general types of human action (pushing, walking, climbing, running, etc.). When men turned from the naming and classifying of actions to that of natural objects, the very generality and elasticity of these concepts permitted their application to forces for which they were not originally designed. The

---

20. Durkheim provides a brief survey (pp. 89–91) of the literature here, but takes the work of F. Max Müller (1823–1900) as paradigmatic. Cf. Müller's *Oxford Essays* (1856), *The Origin and Development of Religion* (1878), *Natural Religion* (1889), *Physical Religion* (1890), *Anthropological Religion* (1892), *Theosophy, or Psychological Religion* (1893), and *Contributions to the Science of Mythology* (1897).

earliest classes of natural phenomena were thus metaphors for human action—a river was "something that moves steadily," the wind was "something that sighs or whistles," etc.—and as these metaphors came to be taken literally, natural forces were quite naturally conceived as the product of powerful, personal agents. Once these agents had received names, the names themselves raised questions of interpretation for succeeding generations, producing the efflorescence of fables, genealogies, and myths characteristic of ancient religions. Finally, the ancestor cult, according to this theory, is purely a secondary development—unable to face the fact of death, men postulated their possession of an immortal soul which, upon separation from the body, was gradually drawn into the circle of divine beings, and eventually deified (1912: 91–97).

Despite the contrast mentioned above, Durkheim's objections to this naturistic hypothesis followed much the same line as those objections to its animistic counterpart. Leaving aside the numerous criticisms of the philological premises of the naturistic theory, Durkheim insisted that nature is characterized not by phenomena so extraordinary as to produce a religious awe, but by a regularity which borders on monotony. Moreover, even if natural phenomena were sufficient to produce a certain degree of admiration, this still would not be equivalent to those features which characterize the "sacred", and least of all to that "absolute duality" which typifies its relations with the "profane." The primitive, in any case, does not regard such forces as superior to his own; on the contrary, he thinks he can manipulate them to his own advantage by the exercise of certain religious rites. And in fact, the earliest objects of such rites were not the principal forms of nature at all, but rather humble animals and vegetables with whom even the primitive man could feel himself at least an equal (1912: 103–105).

Durkheim's major objection, however, was that the naturistic theory, like animism, would reduce religion to little more than a system of hallucinations. It is true, he admitted, that primitive peoples reflect upon the forces of nature from an early period, for they depend on these forces for their very survival. For precisely this reason, however, these forces and the reflections upon them could hardly be the source of religious ideas; for such ideas provide a palpably misleading conception of the nature of such forces, so that any course of practical activity based upon them would surely be unsuccessful, and this in turn would undermine one's faith in the ideas themselves. Again, the important place granted to religious ideas throughout history and in all societies is evidence that they respond to some reality, and one other than that of physical nature (1912: 97–102).

Totemism

Whether from dreams or from physical nature, therefore, animism and naturism both attempt to construct the idea of the sacred out of the facts of our common, individual experience; and for Durkheim, whose argument again parallels Kant's attack on empiricist ethics, such an enterprise is simply impossible: "A fact of common experience," he insisted, "cannot give us the idea of something whose characteristic is to be outside the world of common experience" (1912: 106). Durkheim's largely negative assessment of rival theories of religious origins thus led to his first positive conclusion: "Since neither man nor nature have of themselves a sacred character," he argued,

> they must get it from another source. Aside from the human individual and the physical world, there should be some other reality, in relation to which this variety of delirium which all religion is in a sense, has a significance and an objective value. In other words, beyond those which we have called animistic and naturistic, there should be another sort of cult, more fundamental and more primitive, of which the first are only derived forms or particular aspect. (1912: 107)

This more fundamental and primitive cult is totemism.

The peculiar set of beliefs and practices known as totemism had been discovered among American Indians as early as 1791; and though repeated observations for the next eighty years increasingly suggested that the institution enjoyed a certain generality, it continued to be seen as a largely American, and rather archaic, phenomenon. J.F. McLennan's articles on "The Worship of Animals and Plants" (1870–71) showed that totemism was not only a religion, but one from which considerably more advanced religions had derived; and L.H. Morgan's *Ancient Society* (1877) revealed that this religion was intimately connected to that specific form of social organization that Durkheim had discussed in *The Division of Labor*—the division of the social group into clans. As the same religion and social organization were increasingly observed and reported among the Australian aborigines, the documents accumulated until James Frazer brought them together in *Totemism* (1887). But Frazer's work was purely descriptive, making no effort to understand or explain the most fundamental aspects of totemism. The pivotal work in the explanation and interpretation of this institution, therefore, was Robertson Smith's *Lectures on the Religion of the Semites* (1889), which made totemism the origin of sacrifice, and thus of the ritual apparatus of higher religions generally; and in *The Golden Bough* (1890), Smith's protégé Frazer connected the same ideas to the gods of classical antiquity and the folklore of European peasants. All these works, however, were constructed out of fragmentary observations, for a true totemic religion had not yet been observed in its complete state. This hiatus was filled, however, in Baldwin Spencer and F.J. Gillen's *Native Tribes of Central Australia* (1899), a study of totemic clans almost definitively primitive; and, together with the studies they stimulated, these observations were incorporated within Frazer's four-volume compendium, *Totemism and Exogamy* (1910).

The initial contribution of *The Elementary Forms* to this rapidly growing literature was simply its methodological approach. As a member of the "anthropological" school, for example, Frazer had made no effort to place the various religious systems he studied within their social and historical context; rather, as the name of the school implies, he assumed that man has some sort of innate, religious "nature" regardless of social conditions, and thus "compared" the most disparate beliefs and rites with an eye to their most superficial similarities.[21] But for the sociologist, Durkheim emphasized, social facts vary with the social system of which they are a part, and cannot be understood when detached from that system. For this reason, two facts from different societies cannot be usefully compared simply because they seem to resemble one another; in addition, the societies themselves should resemble each other—be varieties of the same species (cf. 1895: 108–118). Moreover, since the number of societies with which a sociologist can be genuinely familiar is quite limited, and since, in any case, he regarded the alleged "universality" of totemism as a question of only residual interest,

21. Durkheim admitted that *Totemism and Exogamy* (1910) represented some progress away from such a view; for, by setting the domestic institutions of each tribe within their geographic and social environments, Frazer there departed from "the old methods of the anthropological school" (1912: 113 n. 32).

Durkheim ultimately concentrated on the aboriginal societies of central Australia almost exclusively.[22] These societies, indeed, suited Durkheim's purposes admirably—the ethnographic reports of their totemic institutions were easily the most complete, their structural features were all of a single type (the "single-segment" societies of *The Division of Labor* and *The Rules*), and, since this type of societal organization was the most rudimentary known, it seemed to Durkheim the best place to search for that "most primitive" religion whose description and explanation was the central purpose of *The Elementary Forms*.

TOTEMIC BELIEFS: THEIR NATURE, CAUSES, AND CONSEQUENCES

But where, in such totemic societies, was one to look first? At their rites, as had Robertson Smith and the early Frazer? Or at their beliefs, following Tylor and Frazer's later work? The fact that myths are frequently constructed after the rite in order to account for it suggested the first; while recognition that rites are often the sole expression of antecedent beliefs argued for the second.[23] On this contemporary controversy in the scientific study of religion, Durkheim ultimately leaned heavily toward the second alternative; and on the ground that it is impossible to understand a religion without a firm grasp of its ideas, his discussion of Australian totemism in *The Elementary Forms* thus began with its beliefs (1912: 121).

The most fundamental of these beliefs is that the members of each clan[24] consider themselves bound together by a special kind of kinship, based not on blood, but on the mere fact that they share the same name. This name, moreover, is taken from a determined species of material objects (an animal, less frequently a plant, and in rare cases an inanimate object) with which the clan members are

22. Durkheim did not deny himself occasional comparisons with the totemic institutions of the North American Indians, whose clarity, stability, and more advanced stage of development allowed him some rather speculative reconstructions of the historical evolution of totemism (cf. 1912: 115–117). Durkheim's method was thus quite similar to that of Robertson Smith, whose focus was almost exclusively on Semitic religions.

23. Cf. n. 12 above.

24. Australian clans are also joined together in "phratries" which have their own totems, and which Durkheim regarded as former clans (cf. 1912: 128–130).

assumed to enjoy the same relations of kinship. But this "totem" is not simply a name; it is also an emblem, which, like the heraldic coats-of-arms, is carved, engraved, or designed upon the other objects belonging to the clan, and even upon the bodies of the clan members themselves. Indeed, it is these designs which seem to render otherwise common objects "sacred," and their inscription upon the bodies of clan members indicates the approach of the most important religious ceremonies.

The same religious sentiments aroused by these designs, of course, are aroused by the members of the totemic species themselves. Clan members are thus forbidden to kill or eat the totemic animal or plant except at certain mystical feasts (see below), and the violation of this interdiction is assumed to produce death instantaneously. Moreover, the clan members themselves are "sacred" in so far as they belong to the totemic species, a belief which gives rise to genealogical myths explaining how men could have had animal and even vegetable ancestors. Durkheim thus rejected McLennan's interpretation of totemism as a form of animal worship; for man belongs to the sacred world himself, and thus his relations with his totem are much more like those uniting members of the same family (1912: 156–163).

Totemism is thus a religion in which three classes of things—the totemic emblem, the animal or plant, and the members of the clan—are recognized as sacred; but in addition, totemism constitutes a cosmology, in which all known things are distributed among the various clans and phratries,[25] so that everything is classified according to the social organization of the tribe.[26] In short, because men themselves are organized socially, they are able to organize things according to their societal model; thus one of the essential "categories of the understanding"—the idea of class—appears to be the product of certain forms of social organization.[27] But this is not merely a logical or cognitive classification; it is also moral—all things arranged in the same clan are regarded as extensions of the totemic animal, as "of the same flesh," and thus as themselves "sacred" in

25. Cf. n. 24 above.

26. Durkheim and his nephew, Marcel Mauss, had developed this argument in much greater detail in *Primitive Classification* (1903).

27. Durkheim did not deny that the individual intellect can perceive similarities and differences among various objects, but he did deny that such vague, fluctuating images are themselves sufficient to the idea of class, which is the more concrete framework within which such images are distributed (cf. 1912: 170–172).

some degree.[28] Finally, since all of these beliefs clearly imply a division of things between sacred and profane, we may call them "religious"; and since they appear not only related, but inseparably connected, to the simplest form of social organization known, Durkheim insisted that they are surely the most elementary forms of the religious life.

How, then, were these beliefs to be explained?[29] The first step toward an answer to this question, Durkheim suggested, is to recognize that, while all the things discussed above (emblems, animals, clan members, and all other objects) are sacred in different degrees (their sacredness declines in roughly that order), they are all sacred in the same way; thus, their religious character could hardly be due to the special properties of one or the other, but rather is derived from some common principle shared (albeit, again, in different degrees) by all. Totemism, in short, is not a religion of emblems or animals or men at all, but rather of an anonymous, impersonal "force,"[30] immanent in the world and diffused among its various material objects.

But, surely, such a conception surpasses the limits of the primitive mind? On the contrary, Durkheim argued, whether it is described as *mana*, *wakan*, or *orenda*, this belief in a diffused, impersonal force is found among the Samoans, the Melanesians, various North American Indian tribes, and (albeit less abstracted and generalized) among the totemic clans of central Australia.[31] Indeed, this explains why it has

28. To these beliefs, Durkheim added descriptions of "individual totemism" and "sexual totemism," which he regarded as secondary, derivative forms (cf. 1912: 183–193).

29. Durkheim paved the way for his own explanation with a characteristic argument by elimination, in which competing accounts of the origin of totemism (including those of Tylor, G.A. Wilken, Wilhelm Wundt, F.B. Jevons, Frazer, Hill Tout, Alice Fletcher, Franz Boas, and Andrew Lang) were successively taken up, criticized, and discarded. The argument is fascinating in itself and provided a superb example of Durkheim's dialectical virtuosity; but to do justice to it here would require an extended and, in relation to the mainline of Durkheim's argument, unjustified digression (cf. 1912: 195–215).

30. This is not intended metaphorically. Whether construed physically (it can mechanically produce physical effects) or morally (the individuals sharing it feel mutually bound to one another), this principle behaves like a real "force" (cf. 1912: 218–219).

31. Durkheim insisted that an additional "presumption of objectivity" is provided by the multiple, independent, and almost simultaneous discovery of the same conception by a variety of scholars, including R.R. Marett, Hubert and Mauss, Karl Preuss, and even Frazer himself (cf. 1912: 230–232).

been impossible to define religion in terms of mythical personalities, gods, or spirits; for these particular religious things are simply individualized forms of this more impersonal religious principle, and their sacredness is thus non-intrinsic. And quite aside from its purely religious significance, Durkheim argued that this was the original form under which the modern, scientific idea of force was conceived (1912: 232–234).

To explain totemism is thus to explain this belief in a diffused, impersonal force. How might such a belief arise? Obviously, not from sensations aroused by the totemic objects themselves, Durkheim argued, for these objects—the caterpillar, the ant, the frog, etc.—are hardly of a kind to inspire powerful religious emotions; on the contrary, these objects appear to be the symbols or material expressions of something else. Of what, then, are they the symbols? Durkheim's initial answer was that they symbolize both the "totemic principle" and the totem clan; but if this is the case, then surely that principle and the clan are one and the same thing: "The god of the clan, the totemic principle," he insisted, "can therefore be nothing else than the clan itself, personified and represented to the imagination under the visible form of the animal or vegetable which serves as totem" (1912: 236).

This hypothesis—that god is nothing more than society apotheosized—was supported by a number of characteristically Durkheimian arguments. It was insisted, for example, that a society has all that is necessary to arouse the idea of the divine, for it is to its members what a god is to his worshippers. It is both physically and morally superior to individuals, and thus they both fear its power and respect its authority; but society cannot exist except in and through the individual *conscience*, and thus it both demands our sacrifices and periodically strengthens and elevates the divine "principle" within each of us—especially during periods of collective enthusiasm, when its power is particularly perceptible (1912: 236–245). Indeed, it is during such extremely rare gatherings of the entire Australian clan, Durkheim suggested, that the religious idea itself seems to have been born, a fact which explained why its most important religious ceremonies continue to be observed only periodically, when the clan as a whole is assembled. It is this succession of intense periods of "collective effervescence" with much longer periods of dispersed, individualistic economic activity, Durkheim suggested, which gives rise to the belief that there are two worlds—the sacred and the profane—both within us and within nature itself (1912: 245–251).

But how does this belief give rise to totemism? Briefly, the individual who is transported from his profane to a sacred existence in a gathering of the clan seeks some explanation for his altered, elevated state. The gathering of the clan itself is the real cause, though one too complex for the primitive mind to comprehend; but all around him, the clan member sees symbols of precisely that cause—the carved engraved images of the totem—and fixes his confused social sentiments on these clear, concrete objects, from which the physical power and moral authority of society thus seem to emanate. Just as the soldier who dies for his flag in fact dies for his country, so the clan member who worships his totem in fact worships his clan.

To the classical formula *Primus in orbe deos fecit timor*—the fear-theory defended in various ways by Hume, Tylor, and Frazer—Durkheim thus added a decisive, if not entirely original, dissent. Following Robertson Smith—indeed, it was probably this idea, seized upon in his anti-Frazerian mood of 1900, that so dramatically altered Durkheim's conception of religion itself[32]—Durkheim insisted that the primitive man does not regard his gods as hostile, malevolent, or fearful in any way whatsoever; on the contrary, his gods are friends and relatives, who inspire a sense of confidence and well-being. The sense thus inspired, moreover, is not an hallucination, but is based on reality; for however misunderstood, there actually is a real moral power—society—to which these beliefs correspond, and from which the worshipper derives his strength (1912: 255–262).

This argument—the very heart of *The Elementary Forms*[33]—was also intimately bound to Durkheim's important conception of the role of symbols in society. Their utilitarian value as expressions of social sentiments notwithstanding, Durkheim's more ambitious claim was that such symbols serve to *create* the sentiments themselves. For collective representations, as we have seen, presuppose the mutual reaction of individual minds upon one another, reactions inexplicable in the absence of collective symbols; and, once formed, such

32. I have developed this argument at much greater length in: "'Un Homme qui peut davantage': Durkheim and the 'Dynamogenic' Quality of Religion" (Jones, 1985).

33. Cf., for example, Durkheim's defence of the "two principal ideas" of this work before the Société française de philosophie, transcribed and published as "Le Problème religieux et la dualité de la nature humaine" (1913).

representations would quickly dissipate in the absence of symbols which serve to *maintain* them in the individual mind. Thus, society, "in all its aspects and in every period of its history, is made possible only by a vast symbolism" (1912: 264).[34]

This explanation of totemism in turn helps us to understand a phenomenon that had recently been discussed by Lucien Lévy-Bruhl in *Les Fonctions mentales dans les sociétés inférieures* (1910)[35]—that "law of participation" whereby primitive peoples ignore the distinctions between animals, vegetables, and inanimate objects, granting rocks a sex, for example, or a star a soul, thus giving rise to elaborate mythologies in which each being partakes of the properties of others. Inexplicable on the basis of ordinary experience—nowhere do we see beings "mixing their natures" or "metamorphizing themselves into each other"—such participation was explained by Durkheim as a consequence of the symbolic representations just described: once the clan became "represented" by a species of animal or plant, the latter were thought of as relative of men, and both were assumed to "participate in the same nature" (1912: 269).

Finally, like the concept of *mana*, this notion of "participation" had significance for the evolution of scientific as well as purely religious thought. To say that one thing is the cause of another, Durkheim explained, is to establish relations between them, to suggest that they are bound together by some natural, internal law. Like Hume, Durkheim insisted that sensations alone can never disclose such law-like connections; and like Kant, therefore, he argued that the human reason must supply them, thus enabling us to understand cause and effect as necessary relations. The great achievement of primitive religion, Durkheim then suggested, is that it constructed the first representation (the "law of participation") of what these "relations of kinship" might be, thus rescuing man from his enslavement to mere appearance, and rendering science and philosophy possible; and religion could do this, he added, only because it is a mode of *collective* thought, which imposes a new way of representing reality for the old manipulation of purely individual sensations. Between religion and science, Durkheim thus concluded, there can be no abyss; for, while the former applies its logical

34. The choice of animals and vegetables as the particular symbols of totemic clans are explained by their economic importance, their constant proximity and familiarity, and the ease with which they can be represented (cf. 1912: 266).

35. Translated by L. A. Close as *How Natives Think* (1923).

mechanisms to nature more awkwardly than the latter, both are made up of the same collective representations.[36]

Throughout his discussion of the nature and causes of totemic beliefs, Durkheim insisted that no idea of the soul, spirits, or gods plays any role. In order to complete this discussion, therefore, it was necessary to show how such ideas—universal among the known religions—could have evolved out of "the more essential conceptions" just described. Every known society, for example, acknowledges the existence of the human soul—a second, ethereal self, which dwells within and animates the body; and since the Australian aborigines provide the most primitive instance of this belief, Durkheim's search for its origin began by asking how the aborigines themselves explained it.

According to the Australians, Durkheim observed, the souls which enter and animate the bodies of new-born children are not "special and original creations"; on the contrary, they are the old souls of dead ancestors of the clan, whose reincarnation explains the phenomena of conception and birth. To such ancestors superhuman powers and virtues are attributed, rendering them sacred; and most important, they are conceived under the form not of men, but of animals and plants. Durkheim thus concluded that the human soul is simply a form of "individualized *mana*," the totemic principle incarnate, and the most primitive form of that conception of the "duality of human nature" which has perplexed the philosophers and theologians of more advanced societies for centuries.

The last point is important, for Durkheim claimed that this explanation of the belief in the soul helps us to understand two more advanced ideas: the theological conception of *immortality*, and the philosophical idea of *personality*. The first belief, Durkheim argued, cannot be accounted for by the moral demand for a future, just, retribution,[37] for primitive peoples make no such demand; neither can it be explained by the desire to escape to death,[38] an event to

36. In *Les Fonctions mentales*, Lévy-Bruhl had argued that the representations of primitives are emotional and mystical rather than intellectual, and that primitive thought is thus "prelogical," indifferent to modern conceptions of self-contradiction and causality. Durkheim's response, of course, insisted that the differences of primitive and modern thought are those of degree (e.g., more care in observation, more method in explanation) rather than kind, and that the former is the evolutionary origin of the latter (cf. 1912: 270–271).

37. Cf. Kant's *Critique of Practical Reason* (1788) and *Critique of Judgment* (1790).

38. Cf. Hume's "On the Immortality of the Soul" (1777).

which the primitive is relatively indifferent, and from which, in any case, his particular notion of immortality would offer little relief; and finally, it cannot be explained by the appearance of dead relatives and friends in our dreams,[39] an occurrence too infrequent to account for so powerful and prevalent a belief. The failure of these explanations, Durkheim added, is particularly embarrassing in that the idea of the soul itself does not seem to imply its own survival, but rather seems to exclude it—since the soul is intimately connected with the body, the death of the latter would seem to bode ill for the former. This embarrassment is relieved, however, if one accepts Durkheim's explanation, in which the belief in the immortality of the soul and its subsequent reincarnations is literally required if the phenomena of conception and birth are to be explained. And in holding this belief, Durkheim again asserted, the primitive is not misled; for the soul is simply the individualized representation of the clan, and the clan does outlive its individual members. The belief in the immortality of the soul is thus the earliest, symbolic means whereby men represented to themselves the truth that society continued to live while they must die (1912: 303–304).

The philosophical idea of personality would seem to have posed greater difficulties for Durkheim; for the modern notion of what is "personal" seems to imply what is "individual"—an association which would surely confound any sociological explanation. But Durkheim insisted that the terms were in no way synonymous, a distinction clearly evident in their most sophisticated philosophical formulations. In his suggestion that all reality is composed of "monads," for example, Leibniz had emphasized that these psychic entities are personal, conscious, autonomous beings; but he had also insisted that these consciousnesses all express the same world; and, since this world is itself but a system of representations, each particular consciousness is but the reflection of the universal consciousness, the particularity of its perspective being explained by its special location within the whole.[40] Similarly, for Kant, the cornerstone of the personality was the will, that faculty responsible for acting in conformity with the utterly impersonal reason; and to act in accordance with reason was to transcend all that is "individual"

39. Cf. Tylor's *Primitive Culture* (1871).
40. Leibniz's theory of "monads," developed after 1695, can be found in Philip P. Wiener (ed.), *Leibniz: Selections*. New York: Charles Scribner's Sons, 1951, pp. 533–552.

within us (our senses, appetites, inclinations, etc.).[41] For both Leibniz and Kant, therefore, a "person" was less an individual subject distinguished from all others than a being enjoying a relative autonomy in relation to its immediate environment; but this, Durkheim concluded, is precisely the description of the primitive idea of the soul—that individualized form of society within, yet independent of, the body (1912: 305–308).

The subsequent evolution of totemic beliefs is one from souls to spirits, spirits to "civilizing heroes," and heroes to "high gods," in which the focus of religious worship becomes increasingly powerful, personal, and international. Since the idea of souls is inexplicable without postulating original, "archetypal" souls from which the others are derived, for example, the primitive imagines mythical ancestors or "spirits" at the beginning of time, who are the source of all subsequent religious efficacy.[42] When the clans come together for the tribal initiation ceremonies, the primitive similarly seeks an explanation for the homogeneity and generality of the rites thus performed; and the natural conclusion is that each group of identical ceremonies was founded by one great ancestor, the "civilizing hero" of the clan, who is now venerated by the larger tribe as well.[43] And where the tribe as a whole, gathered at such initiation ceremonies, acquires a particularly powerful sentiment of itself, some symbol of this sentiment is sought; as a result, one of the heroes is elevated into a "high god," whose authority is recognized not only by the tribe thus inspired, but by many of its neighbors. The result is a truly "international" deity, whose attributes bear a marked similarity to those of the higher religions of more advanced civilizations.[44] But this "great tribal god," Durkheim emphasized, retracing his evolutionary steps, "is only an ancestral spirit who finally won a pre-eminent place. The ancestral spirits are only entities forged in the image of the individual souls whose origin they are destined to explain. The souls, in their turn, are only the form taken by the impersonal forces which

41. Again, cf. Kant's *Critique of Practical Reason* (1788).

42. Durkheim suggested that this is the explanation for what he, and Frazer before him, had called "individual totemism" (cf. 1912: 315–316).

43. This is a clear example of Durkheim's application of the "ritual theory of myth," first proposed by Robertson Smith.

44. For example, such gods are considered immortal, eternal, and providential; as the "creators" of all living beings; as having lived on earth themselves, before ascending into "heaven"; and as moral judges, even prophesying a "judgment day" on which good and evil men will receive their appropriate deserts (cf. 1912: 322–326).

we found at the basis of totemism, as they individualize themselves in the human body. The unity of the system," Durkheim concluded, "is as great as its complexity" (1912: 332–333).

TOTEMIC RITES: THEIR NATURE AND CAUSES

Despite an occasional dalliance with the ritual theory of myth,[45] Durkheim's most consistent position was that the cult depends upon the beliefs; but he also insisted that beliefs and rites are inseparable, not only because the rites are often the sole manifestation of otherwise imperceptible ideas, but also because they react upon and thus alter the nature of the ideas themselves. Having completed his extensive analysis of the nature, causes, and consequences of totemic beliefs, therefore, Durkheim turned to a somewhat shorter discussion of the "principal ritual attitudes" of totemism.

Sacred things, as we have seen, are those rather dramatically separated from their profane counterparts; and a substantial group of totemic rites has as its object the realization of this essential state of separation. In so far as these rites merely prohibit certain actions or impose certain abstentions, they consist entirely of interdictions or "taboos";[46] and thus Durkheim described the system formed by these rites as the "negative cult."[47] The interdictions characterizing these rites were in turn divided into two classes: those separating the sacred from the profane, and those separating sacred things from one another according to their "degree of sacredness";[48] and even the

---

45. See n. 43 above.

46. Here, with significant reservations (cf. 1912: 338), Durkheim adopted the common idiom inaugurated by Frazer's *Encyclopedia Britannica* article "Taboo" (1887).

47. Consistent with his earlier, rather *ad hoc*, distinction, Durkheim's analysis of the negative cult explicitly avoided any discussion of those interdictions associated with magic. Two reasons were offered: first, while both magical and religious interdictions pre-suppose sanctions which follow violations of the interdict *automatically*, religious interdictions presuppose additional sanctions imposed by human agents; and second, while the objects to which magical interdictions are applied are kept separate as the consequence of fear, those to which religious interdictions are applied are kept separate out of respect for their "sacredness." To use the Kantian terminology, magical interdictions are hypothetical imperatives, while religious interdictions are categorical.

48. Many of the second type, Durkheim observed, can be traced back to the first (cf. 1912: 340 n. 7).

first class alone assumes a variety of forms—certain foods are forbidden to profane persons because they are sacred, while others are forbidden to sacred persons because they are profane; certain objects cannot be touched or even looked at; certain words or sounds cannot be uttered; and certain activities, particularly those of an economic or utilitarian character, are forbidden during periods when religious ceremonies are being performed. For all their diversity, however, Durkheim argued that all these forms are reducible to two fundamental interdictions: the religious life and the profane life cannot coexist in the same place, and they cannot coexist in the same unit of time.

Although literally defined in terms of these interdictions, however, the negative cult also exercises a "positive" function—it is the condition of access to the positive cult. Precisely because of the abyss which separates sacred things from their profane counterparts, the individual cannot enter into relations with the first without ridding himself of the second. In the initiation ceremony, for example, the neophyte is submitted to a large variety of negative rites whose net effect is to produce a radical alteration of his moral and religious character, to "sanctify" him through his suffering, and ultimately to admit him to the sacred life of the clan. But here, again, religion is only the symbolic form of society which, while augmenting our powers and enabling us to transcend ourselves, demands our sacrifice and self-abnegation, suppresses our instincts, and does violence to our natural inclinations. There is a ruthless asceticism in all social life, Durkheim argued, which is the source of all religious asceticism (1912: 355–356).

But if this is the function of the negative cult, what is its cause? In one sense, of course, this system of interdicts is logically implied by the very notion of "sacredness" itself, for respect habitually begets inhibition; but many things acquire and retain our respect without becoming the objects of religious interdictions. The peculiar attribute of sacred things which renders them, in particular, the objects of the negative cult is what Durkheim called "the contagiousness of the sacred"—religious forces easily escape their original locations and flow, almost irresistibly, to any objects within their range. In so doing, of course, they contradict their own essential nature, which is to remain separated from the profane; and thus a whole system of restrictions is necessary in order to keep the two worlds apart (1912: 356–361).

But how was this contagiousness *itself* to be explained?[49] Observing that such contagiousness is characteristic of those forces or properties (heat, electricity, etc.) which enter a body *from without* rather than being intrinsic to it, Durkheim reminded his reader that this is precisely what his own theory implies—religious forces do not inhere in physical nature, but rather are brought to it by the collective representations of society. Indeed, it is by an initial "act of contagion" (see above) that ordinary objects receive their sacred character in the first place; and it is natural that, in the absence of rigorous interdictions, they should lose this character just as easily.[50]

This brings us to the most crucial phase of Durkheim's treatment of totemic rites, that based upon those materials which, in the 1899–1901 period, so dramatically altered his understanding of religion.[51] Until 1899, as Durkheim himself observed, the negative cult just described was virtually all that was known of the religious aspect of totemism; but the negative cult, as we have seen, contains no reason for existing in itself, and merely introduces the individual to more positive relations with sacred things. The significance of Spencer and Gillen's *Native Tribes of Central Australia* (1899), therefore, was that it described one ceremony in particular that exhibits the essential features of the "positive cult" found in more advanced religions—the Arunta *Intichiuma* ceremony.

In central Australia, Durkheim explained, there are two sharply divided seasons: one is long and dry, the other short and very rainy. When the second arrives, the vegetation springs up from the ground, the animals multiply, and what had been a sterile desert abounds with

49. Durkheim briefly entertained the hypothesis proposed by F.B. Jevons in his *Introduction to the History of Religions* (1896), which emphasized the association of ideas. The difficulty for Jevons's argument, Durkheim observed, is not simply that civilized men, who continue to honor sacred objects, would be unlikely to be deceived by such associations; more important, primitive men themselves seem equally undeceived in all but their most *religious* preoccupations. The special status of the latter thus remains untouched by any purely psychological hypothesis (cf. 1912: 361–362).

50. This, of course, is Durkheim's explanation for that "law of participation" observed by Lévy-Bruhl (cf. 1912: 365, and above).

51. Durkheim himself said that his "*révélation*" came in 1895, upon his reading of the works of "Robertson Smith and his school"; but, as I have argued in "Un Homme qui peut davantage" (Jones, 1985), Smith's influence is evident in Durkheim's work only after 1900, when he attempted to countermand Frazer's interpretation of Spencer and Gillen's observations of the Arunta *Intichiuma*. This surely led him *back* to Smith, whose views he then grasped for the first time (cf. Durkheim, 1902b, and n. 32 above).

luxurious flora and fauna; and it is at the moment when this "good" season seems near at hand that the *Intichiuma* is celebrated. Every totemic clan has its own *Intichiuma*, and the celebration itself has two phases. The object of the first is to assure the abundance of that animal or plant which serves as the clan's totem, an object obtained by striking together certain sacred stones (sometimes drenched with the blood of clan members), thus detaching and scattering grains of dust which assure the fertility of the animal or plant species. The second phase begins with an intensification of the interdictions of the negative cult—clan members who could ordinarily eat their totemic animal or plant if they did so in moderation now find that it cannot be eaten or even touched—and concludes with a solemn ceremony in which representatives of the newly increased totemic species are ritually slaughtered and eaten by the clan members, after which the exceptional interdictions are lifted and the clan returns to its normal existence (1912: 368–377).

To Durkheim, the significance of this system of rites was that it seemed to contain the essential elements of the most fundamental rite of the higher religions—sacrifice; and equally important, it seemed in large part to confirm the revolutionary theory of the meaning of that rite put forward by Robertson Smith twenty-four years earlier.[52] The more traditional theory of sacrifice, epitomized in Tylor's *Primitive Culture* (1871), was that the earliest offerings were "gifts" presented to the god by his worshippers; but such a theory, Durkheim observed, failed to account for two important features of the rite: that its substance was food, and that this food was shared by both gods and worshippers at a common feast. Noting that in many societies such commensality is believed to create (and re-create) a bond of kinship, Smith had suggested that the earliest sacrifices were less acts of renunciation and expiation than joyous feasts, in which the bond of kinship uniting gods and worshippers was periodically reaffirmed by participation in the common flesh.

Insisting (*pace* Smith) that it was participation in *sacred* flesh that rendered the rite efficacious, Durkheim argued that the ceremony concluding the second phase of the *Intichiuma* was precisely such a rite; and in the Australian rite, he added, the object of such communion was clear—the periodic revivification of that "totemic

52. Cf. Smith's *Encyclopedia Britannica* article "Sacrifice" (1886), as well as the more detailed statement of the theory in his *Lectures on the Religion of the Semites* (1889).

principle" (society) which exists within each member of the clan and is symbolized by the sacrificial animal or plant. This in turn explained the temporal aspect of the rite—the totemic principle would seem most thoroughly exhausted after a long, dry period, and most completely renewed just after the arrival of the "good season"; and analogous practices were found among many, more advanced peoples: ". . . the *Intichiuma* of the Australian societies," Durkheim concluded, "is closer to us than one might imagine from its apparent crudeness" (1912: 380).

But if Durkheim shared Smith's view that the earliest sacrifices were acts of communion, he did not share his view that this was *all* they were, nor did he share Smith's reasons for holding these views in the first place. For Smith was a devout Scottish Calvinist who found the very idea that the gods receive physical pleasure from the offerings of mere mortals a "revolting absurdity", and insisted that this conception had no part in the original meaning of the rite, emerging only much later with the institution of private property.[53] In the first phase of the *Intichiuma*, however, Durkheim found precisely this idea—the totemic species requires the performance of certain rites in order to reproduce itself—and thus he suggested that the complete sacrifice is both an offering and a communion (1912: 381–385).

To Durkheim, moreover, this was not a minor, antiquarian quibble, for his subsequent explanation of this "mutual interdependence" of gods and worshippers was a major part of his sociological theory of religion. We have already seen, for example, how the "logic" of the *Intichiuma* corresponds to the intermittent character of the *physical* environment of central Australia—long dry spells punctuated by heavy rainfall and the reappearance of animals and vegetation. This intermittency, Durkheim now added, is duplicated by the *social* life of the Australian clans—long periods of dispersed, individual economic activity, punctuated by the intensive communal activity of the *Intichiuma* itself.[54] Since sacred beings exist only at the sufferance of collective representations, we should expect that their

53. Smith (1889: 392–396). The idea of private property, Smith observed (1889: 396) "materializes everything that it touches . . . ."

54. While the social environment thus "duplicates" the periodicity of its physical counterpart, Durkheim hardly granted them equal status in his explanation. The fluctuations of physical nature merely provide the "occasions" upon which men assemble or disperse, the "outer framework" within which the truly determinative action of society operates (cf. 1912: 391).

presence would be most deeply felt precisely when men gather to worship them, when they "partake of the same idea and the same sentiment"; in a sense, therefore, the Australian was not mistaken— the gods *do* depend upon their worshippers, even as the worshippers depend upon their gods, for society can exist only in and through individuals, even as the individual gets from society the best part of himself (1912: 385–392).

In addition to this primitive form of sacrifice, Durkheim discussed three other types of positive rites—imitative, representative, and piacular—which either accompany the *Intichiuma* or, in some tribes, replace it altogether. The first consists of movements and cries whose function, guided by the principle that "like produces like", is to imitate the animal or plant whose reproduction is desired. These rites had been interpreted by the "anthropological school" (Tylor and Frazer) as a kind of "sympathetic magic," to be explained, as in Jevons's account of the contagiousness of the sacred,[55] by the association of ideas; and as it had been to Jevons, Durkheim's response to Tylor and Frazer was that a specific, concrete social phenomenon cannot be explained by a general, abstract law of psychology. Indeed, restored to their actual context, Durkheim argued, imitative rites are fully explained by the fact that the clan members feel that they really *are* the animal or plant of their totemic species, that this is their most essential trait, and that this should be demonstrated whenever the clan gathers. In fact, it is only on the basis of such demonstrations that the *Intichiuma* could have the revivifying efficacy which Durkheim attributed to it.[56] Far from being a magical, utilitarian rite to be explained by psychology, Durkheim concluded, the imitative rite was a moral, religious phenomenon to be explained sociologically (1912: 393–405).[57]

The principle "like produces like" thus has its origin in collective representations rather than the association of ideas in the individual mind, a fact of as much interest to the history of science as to the history of religion and magic; for Durkheim insisted that this principle was itself a primitive version of the more recent, scientific law of causality. Consider the two essential elements of that law:

55. Cf. 49 above.

56. For this reason, Durkheim eventually concluded that imitative rites were the earliest form of the cult, from which all other forms were subsequently derived (cf. 1912: 432–433).

57. Durkheim's argument reversed the first two stages of the evolutionary sequence (i.e., magic–religion–science) proposed by Frazer in *The Golden Bough* (1890; 1900), relying heavily on Mauss's *General Theory of Magic* (1904).

first, it presumes the idea of efficacy, of an active force capable of producing some effect; and second, it presupposes an *a priori* judgment that this cause produces its effect *necessarily*. The prototype of the first idea, as we have seen, is that collective force conceived by primitive peoples under the name of *mana, wakan, orenda*, etc., and then objectified and projected into things. The second is explained by the fact that the periodic reproduction of the totemic species is a matter of great concern to the clan, and the rites assumed to effect it are thus obligatory. What is obligatory in action, however, cannot remain optional in thought; thus society imposes a logical precept—like produces like—as an extension of the ritual precept essential to its well-being. Durkheim thus repeated the claim of his introduction—that the sociological theory of the categories could reconcile the *a priorist* with the empiricist epistemology—by showing how their necessity and universality could be both retained and explained: "The imperatives of thought," Durkheim concluded, "are probably only another side to the imperatives of action" (1912: 412).

Nonetheless, throughout Durkheim's discussion of sacrificial and imitative rites, there is a palpable air of insecurity; for the *Intichiuma* gave almost every indication of being precisely what Frazer, Spencer, and Gillen had said that it was—a cooperative system of magic designed to increase the supply of the totemic animal.[58] It was with an almost audible sigh of relief, therefore, that Durkheim turned to those "representative" or "commemorative" rites found in the *Intichiuma* of the Warramunga tribe (but which Durkheim insisted were "implicit" in the Arunta rite as well); for these rites contained no gesture whose object was the reproduction of the totemic species, consisting entirely of dramatic representations designed to recall the mythical history of the clan. But a mythology, Durkheim observed, is a moral system and a cosmology as well a history; thus, "the rite serves and can serve only to sustain the vitality of these beliefs, to keep them from being effaced from memory and, in sum, to revivify the most essential elements of the collective consciousness" (1912: 420). So the efficacy of the rites, again, was moral, religious, and social rather than economic, magical, and material.[59] Indeed,

58. Cf. Frazer's "The Origin of Totemism" (1899).

59. Durkheim acknowledged the fact that many "representative" rites are construed as having the same physical efficacy as their "imitative" counterparts; but he insisted that such interpretations are "accessory" and "contingent", not essential to the rite itself (cf. 1912: 423).

Durkheim insisted that here we see the origin of the aesthetic element in the higher religions—all that is artistic, expressive, and re-creative, rather than economic and utilitarian—which, far from being a trivial accoutrement, plays an essential role in the religious life (cf. 1912: 424–428).

Durkheim concluded his treatment of the positive cult with a discussion of "piacular" rites—those which, in sharp contrast to the confident, joyous celebrations just described, are characterized by sadness, fear, and anger. Such rites ordinarily follow some disaster that has befallen the clan (the death of one of its members), and may involve the knocking out of teeth, severing of fingers, burning of skin, or any number of other self-inflicted tortures; but Durkheim insisted (*pace* Jevons again) that none of these acts were the spontaneous expression of individual emotion. On the contrary, such "mourning" appeared to be a duty imposed by the group and sanctioned by severe penalties, which the primitive says are required by the souls of ancestors; but in fact, Durkheim argued, the obligatory character of these rites is to be explained in the same way as their more joyous counterparts—when someone dies, the clan assembles, thus giving rise to collective representations which reflect its sense of loss while simultaneously reaffirming the sense of its own permanence and solidarity (1912: 442–449).[60]

Finally, this account of piacular rituals also accounted for what Durkheim called the "ambiguity of the sacred." In his *Lectures* (1889), Robertson Smith had already suggested that primitive peoples distinguish not simply between sacred and profane, but also between sacred things which are good, pure, benevolent, and propitious, and those which are evil, impure and malicious, and unpropitious (cf. p. 123 n.14 above); and also that, while these two categories of things are separated like the sacred and the profane, there is also a certain "kinship" between them—they both have the same relations of absolute heterogeneity with respect to profane things, and frequently, through a mere change of external circumstances, an evil, impure sacred thing may be transformed into its good, pure counterpart. But while Smith had an "active sentiment" of this

---

60. Durkheim thus rejected Robertson Smith's view that the sense of sin and expiation was a late product of higher religions, arguing instead that it was implicit in the sentiments of fear and misery which gave rise to the earlier piacular rituals (cf. 1912: 453–455).

ambiguity, Durkheim observed, he never explained it.[61] How are evil forces also sacred? And how are they transformed into their counterparts? Durkheim's answers were that evil powers are the symbolic expression of those collective representations excited by periods of grief or mourning and consequent assemblies of the clan, and that they are transformed into their more benign opposites by that reaffirmation of the permanence and solidarity of the group effected by the ceremonies thus celebrated. These two extremes of the religious life thus reflect the two extremes through which all social life must pass. "So, at bottom," Durkheim concluded, "it is the unity and diversity of social life which make the simultaneous unity and diversity of sacred beings and things" (1912: 460).

THE SOCIAL ORIGINS OF RELIGION AND SCIENCE

Social scientists who have attempted to "explain" religion have typically regarded it as a system of ideas or beliefs, of which the rites are an external, material expression; and this has naturally led to a concern for whether these ideas and beliefs may or may not be reconciled with those of modern science. The difficulty for this approach, Durkheim argued, is that it does not correspond to the religious believer's own account of the nature of his experience, which is less one of thought than of action: "The believer who has communicated with his god," Durkheim observed, "is not merely a man who sees new truths of which the unbeliever is ignorant; he is a man who is *stronger*. He feels within him more force, either to endure the trials of existence, or to conquer them" (1912: 464). The mere ideas of the individual are clearly insufficient to this purpose; and, in this sociological version of the principle *extra ecclesia nulla salus*, Durkheim thus insisted that it is the repeated acts of the cult which give rise to "impressions of joy, of interior peace, of serenity, of enthusiasm which are, for the believer, an experimental proof of his beliefs" (1912: 464).

61. This was not quite fair to Smith, who argued that the difference between gods and demons was that the first enjoyed stable, institutionalized relations with men, while the latter was approached only by individuals for private, asocial purposes; the first was religion, the second, magic (cf. Smith, 1889: 90, 264). Durkheim, for whom magic and sacredness were virtually antithetical categories, could hardly have been attracted by this explanation.

Durkheim thus agreed with William James,[62] who, in *The Varieties of Religious Experience* (1902), had argued that religious beliefs rest upon real experiences whose demonstrative value, though different, is in no way inferior to that of scientific experiments. As with such experiments, Durkheim added, it does not follow that the reality which gives rise to these experiences precisely corresponds to the ideas that believers (or scientists) form of it; but it is a reality just the same, and for Durkheim, the reality was society. This, indeed, explained why the cult rather than the idea is so important in religion—"society cannot make its influence felt unless it is in action, and it is not in action unless individuals who compose it are assembled together and act in common" (1912: 465). But Durkheim also felt that all societies need such periodic reaffirmations of their collective sentiments, and that there is thus something "eternal" in religion, destined to outlive the particular symbols—totemic, Christian, or otherwise—in which it had been previously embodied. The difficulty for a society living through the period of "transition" and "moral mediocrity" described in *The Division of Labor* and *Suicide* was in imagining what form its future symbols might assume.

But if religion is thus a mode of action, it is also a mode of thought—one not different in kind from that exercised by science. Like science, for example, religion reflects on nature, man, and society, attempts to classify things, relates them to one another, and explains them; and as we have seen, even the most essential categories of scientific thought are religious in origin. Scientific thought, in short, is but a more perfect form of religious thought; and Durkheim thus felt that the latter would gradually give way before the inexorable advances of the former, including those advances in the social sciences extending to the scientific study of religion itself. In so far as it remains a mode of *action*, however, religion will endure, albeit under yet unforeseen forms (1912: 474–479).

Science is thus religious in its origins; but if religion is itself only the apotheosis of society, then all logical, scientific thought originates in society. How is this possible? All logical thought, Durkheim explained, is made up of *concepts*—generalized ideas which are distinguished from sensations by two important characteristics. First, they are relatively stable—unlike our sensations, which succeed one

62. Though not with his epistemological views: cf. Durkheim's *Pragmatism and Sociology* (1913–1914).

another in a never-ending flux and cannot repeat themselves, our concepts remain the same for long periods of time. Second, they are impersonal—again unlike our sensations, which are held privately and cannot be communicated, our concepts are not only communicable but provide the necessary means by which all communication becomes possible. These two characteristics in turn reveal the origin of conceptual thought. Since concepts are held in common and bear the mark of no individual mind; they are clearly the products of the collective mind, and if they have greater permanence and stability than our individual sensations, it is because they are collective representations, which respond much more slowly to environmental conditions. It is only through society, therefore, that men become capable of logical thought—indeed, of stable, impersonal "truth" altogether; and this explains why the "correct" manipulation of such concepts carries a *moral* authority unknown to mere personal opinion and private experience (1912: 479–487).

In one sense, the "categories of the understanding" (p. 118 above) are simply concepts so stable and impersonal that they have come to be seen as immutable and universal; but in another sense, the social explanation of the categories is more complex, for they not only *have social causes* but also *express social things*:

the category of class was at first indistinct from the concept of the human group; it is the rhythm of social life which is at the basis of the category of time; the territory occupied by the society furnished the material for the category of space; it is the collective force which was the prototype of the concept of efficient force, an essential element in the category of causality. (1912: 488)

How is it that these categories, the pre-eminent concepts by which all of our knowledge is constructed, have been modeled upon and express social things? Durkheim's answer was that, precisely because the categories must perform this permanent, pre-eminent function, they must be based upon a reality of equally permanent, pre-eminent status—a function for which our shifting, private sensations are clearly inadequate.

It might be argued, of course, that society is also inadequate for this function, that there can be no guarantee, for example, that categories modeled on social things will provide an accurate representation of nature; but this would be to deprive society of those attributes which Durkheim had laboriously attached to it throughout his productive and distinguished career. Society, for example, is itself a part of nature, and since "nature cannot contradict itself" we can expect that categories modeled on its realities will correspond to those of the physical world;[63] and, in so far as the concepts founded in any particular group reflect the peculiarities of its special situation, we can expect that the increasing "internationalization" of social life will purge such concepts of their subjective, personal elements, so that we come closer and closer to truth, not in spite of the influence of society, but because of it (1912: 493).

Like Kant, therefore, Durkheim denied any conflict between science, on the one hand, and morality and religion, on the other; for also like Kant, he felt that both were directed toward universal principles, and that both thus implied that, in thought as in action, man can lift himself above the limitations of his private, individual nature to live a rational, impersonal life. What Kant could not explain (indeed, he refused to do so) is the *cause* of this dual existence that we are forced to lead, torn between the sensible and intelligible worlds which, even as they seem to contradict each other, seem to presume and even require each other as well. But to Durkheim the explanation was clear—we lead an existence which is simultaneously both individual and social, and as individuals we can live without society no more than society can live without us.

CRITICAL REMARKS

Had Durkheim written nothing but *The Elementary Forms*, his place in the history of sociological thought would have been secure. It is a work of stunning theoretical imagination, whose two major themes and more than a dozen provocative hypotheses have stimulated the interest and excitement of several generations of sociologists irrespective of theoretical "school" or field of specialization. Nonetheless, it is not without flaws; indeed, it contains most of the indiscretions discussed earlier, and a few others besides. In sharp contrast to Max Weber, for example, Durkheim largely ignores the role of individual religious leaders, as well as the way religion functions in social conflict and asymmetrical relations of power. The

63. Cf. p. 120 above. Lukes (1972: 440) notes that here Durkheim anticipates both Lévi-Strauss and the early Wittgenstein.

"collective effervescence" stimulated by religious assemblies presumes a social psychology never made explicit, and Durkheim's account of how such gatherings generate totemic symbols is dubious to say the least. His definition of religion, preceded by an extended argument by elimination and containing a massive *petitio principii*, bears little relation to anything that the central Australians themselves understand by their beliefs and behavior; and students of aboriginal religion like W.E.H. Stanner have spent months looking for instances of the sacred–profane dichotomy, even to the point of questioning their own competence, before admitting that the Australian facts simply do not fit (Stanner, 1967: 229).

Indeed, if there is a single feature of the work more disturbing than any other, it is Durkheim's treatment of the ethnographic evidence. The choice of the "single case" of central Australia has an intrinsic appeal to anyone familiar with the "scissors and paste" method of comparative religion epitomized in *The Golden Bough*; but in practice, this focus led Durkheim either to ignore counter-instances among the neighboring Australian tribes, or to interpret them arbitrarily according to some *ad hoc*, evolutionary speculations, or to "correct" them in light of the more advanced, and hence allegedly more edifying, American tribes. In fact, there is no evidence that Australian totemism is the earliest *totemism*, let alone the earliest *religion*; and, though technically less advanced than the North American Indians, the Australians have a kinship system which is far more complex. But then, *pace* Durkheim, there is no necessary relationship between the "simplicity" of a society (however that is defined) and that of their religious beliefs and practices; nor, for that matter, is there any necessary relationship between religion and totemism generally (*wakan* and *mana* have no discernible relationship to the "totemic principle").

Even if we limit ourselves to Australian tribes, we find that the *central* tribes are atypical (the *Intichiuma*, for example, scarcely exists elsewhere, and where it does, its meaning is altogether different); that the major cohesive force among aborigines is the tribe rather than the clan; that there are clans without totems (and totems without clans); that most totems are not represented by the carvings and inscriptions on which Durkheim placed so much weight; and that the "high gods" of Australia are not born of a synthesis of totems.[64]

64. For more detailed accounts of these and other empirical shortcomings, see Lukes (1972: 477–480); and Pickering (1984).

Finally, we may choose to circumvent the details of Durkheim's interpretation of the ethnographic literature altogether, observing that its *raison d'être*—the notion that the "essence" of religion itself may be found among the Arunta—is, in Clifford Geertz's words (1973: 22), "palpable nonsense." What one finds among the Arunta are the beliefs and practices of the Arunta, and even to call these "religious" is to impose the conventions of one's own culture and historical period.

Criticisms such as these have led some scholars[65] to suggest that the Australian data were introduced simply to illustrate Durkheim's theories, rather than the theories being constructed or adopted to account for the data. But this suggestion requires at least one major qualification in the light of what we know about the historical development of Durkheim's ideas on religion. The "largely formal and rather *simpliste*" conception of religion characteristic of Durkheim's early work,[66] for example, persisted at least until the appearance of Baldwin Spencer and F.J. Gillen's *Native Tribes of Central Australia* (1899); and it was the largely psychologistic and utilitarian interpretation of these ethnographic data proposed by Frazer (and endorsed by Spencer himself) which led Durkheim back to the more determinedly sociological (even mystical) views of Robertson Smith, and to the contrived and even grotesque evolutionary interpretation of these data found in "Sur le totémisme" (1902b). If the theories of *The Elementary Forms* do not "explain the facts" of Australian ethnography, therefore, it is because so much of their original purpose was rather to explain them *away*.[67]

The most ambitious claim of *The Elementary Forms*, of course, is that the most basic categories of human thought have their origin in social experience; but this claim, Steven Lukes has argued, is not one but six quite different claims, which Durkheim did not consistently and clearly distinguish—the *heuristic* claim that concepts (including the categories) are collective representations; the *causal* claim that society produces these concepts; the *structuralist* claim that these concepts are modeled upon, and are thus similar to, the structures of

65. Cf., for example, Seger (1957: 69). This interpretation gathers force from the famous story about Durkheim told by Henri Bergson: "When we told him that the facts were in contradiction with his theories," Bergson observed, "he would reply: 'The facts are wrong.'"

66. Cf. Lukes (1972: 240).

67. For a more fully developed account of this argument, see Jones (1985).

society; the *functionalist* claim that logical conformity is necessary to social stability; the *cosmological* claim that religious myth provided the earliest systems of classification; and the *evolutionary* claim that the most fundamental notions of modern science have primitive religious origins. The structuralist, cosmological, and evolutionary claims, Lukes observed, have been both challenging and influential. But the heuristic claim, by conflating the categories with concepts in general, confuses a *capacity* of mind with what is better described as its *content*. In so far as society is literally defined in terms of collective representations (as the later Durkheim increasingly did), both the causal and the functionalist claims seem simply to restate the heuristic claim, and are vulnerable to the same objection; but, in so far as society is construed in structural terms (as in *The Division of Labor*), the causal claim in particular is open to serious objections. The very relations proposed between the structures of primitive societies and their conceptual apparatus, for example, would seem to presuppose the primitives' possession of precisely those concepts; and the causal hypothesis itself cannot be framed in falsifiable form—we cannot postulate a situation in which men do *not* think with such concepts, Lukes observes, because this is what thinking *is*.[68] Finally, Durkheim's sociology of knowledge seems susceptible to at least as many empirical objections as his sociology of religion.[69]

68. Cf. Lukes (1972: 435–449). For a contrasting effort to resurrect Durkheim's argument, however, see Bloor (1984).

69. On these in particular see Needham (1963: vii–xlviii).

Epilogue:
Why Read the Classics?

It has been a full century since, in his first publication—a relatively insignificant review of the first volume of Alfred Schaeffle's *Bau und Leben des sozialen Körpers*—Durkheim suggested that sociology "has now emerged from the heroic age. . . . Let it establish itself," he added, "become organized, draw up its programme and specify its method";[1] and, indeed, sociology has become so thoroughly established, organized, programmatic, and methodologically specific as to relegate Durkheim himself to that antiquarian if "heroic" status from which he felt his discipline had already emerged. Possessed of the full weaponry of advanced multivariate analysis, therefore, the modern student of sociology increasingly asks a disquieting question: Why read Durkheim? Or, for that matter, Weber, or Spencer, or Marx? And aside from the knee-jerk response that the question itself is terrifyingly parochial (and indeed it is), the sociological theorist is increasingly required to produce a somewhat more adequate and compelling answer.

The answer of first resort is typically an appeal to the ongoing utility of the classics, to the argument that they contain much that is still relevant to contemporary sociological theory. Adopting W.G. Runciman's distinction between reportage, explanation, description, and evaluation in sociological theory,[2] for example, we might suggest that, where Durkheim's "report" of what the Australian aborigines are doing in the *Intichiuma* ceremony still seems accurate, we will naturally prefer it to Frazer's report of twelve years earlier, and sociological interest in *The Elementary Forms* will thus be enhanced by contrast to that in the second edition of *The Golden Bough*. Similarly, where Durkheim's explanation of progressive differentia-

1. Quoted in Lukes (1972: 85).
2. Cf. Runciman (1983: 50–54).

tion as the consequence of the increasing volume and density of societies is demonstrably valid, we will surely prefer *The Division of Labor* to Spencer's emphasis, in *Principles of Sociology*, on the influence of diverse physical environments upon an expansive and inherently unstable social mass. While authentic "descriptions" (in Runciman's sense) are rare even in the later Durkheim, the account of "what it is like" to perform a moral action found in "The Determination of the Moral Fact" (1906), with its eudemonistic emphasis, will again be preferred to the descriptively austere focus on obligation alone found in Kant's *Groundwork of the Metaphysic of Morals* (1785). And the admiration felt by sociologists for "Individualism and the Intellectuals" (1898a) is surely the consequence not only of Durkheim's devastating attack on the arguments of Ferdinand Brunetière, but also of the fact that we share the liberal, secular, egalitarian, and Dreyfusard values of the first while rejecting the rightist, militaristic, and anti-Semitic values of the second. Durkheim, in short, is still sufficiently close to us that his problems might be profitably regarded as our problems as well, and we might learn from his solutions accordingly.

The difficulty for such a utilitarian justification for the reading of the classics is that it bears but a limited relation to the larger reasons why sociologists read the classics. Indeed, if we read *The Elementary Forms* only for the accuracy of its reports, the validity of its explanations, the authenticity of its descriptions, and/or the congeniality of its values, then I suspect that we shall soon stop reading it altogether; for, as the "critical remarks" appended to Chapter 5 suggest, those parts which are accurate, valid, authentic, and/or congenial might easily be extracted to form a much shorter, though equally "useful," work. Indeed, especially for writers like Comte and Spencer, whose lights shine less bright, such putatively painless extractions are occasionally performed; but both the apologies with which these appear and the justifiably low regard in which they are held suggest that we also read Durkheim because of his *distance from us*, because in some sense his problems are palpably *not ours*, and because there is still so much more to be learned.

But what *do* we learn? Why should we read those passages of *The Division of Labor* in which Durkheim, determinedly ignorant of the ethnographic literature, overstates the role of repressive law in primitive societies? Why must we understand that Durkheim's distinction between "normal" and "pathological" facts was little more than an effort to grant scientific status to his own social and political preferences? Is it simply interesting—or is it also important—to know that Durkheim's analysis of the relation between religious confessions and suicide is an implicit celebration of Ferry's program for secular education? And why must we take seriously Durkheim's claim that the "essence" of religion itself will be disclosed by the study of the aborigines of central Australia—a claim epitomizing the worst excesses of Victorian anthropology?

 An initial answer is simply that this is what sociological thinking *is*, warts and all, carried out at its most powerful, rarefied, and intellectually demanding level; and for those of us who do it not nearly so well (our advantages over Durkheim are cultural, not intellectual), it is instructive to study the works of those who did it so much better. It is a commonplace of the sociology of knowledge and science, for example, that our societies place formidable (though typically unacknowledged and even unrecognized) constraints on our imaginations; to learn that (and how) Durkheim's own imagination was similarly constrained is thus to learn something about ourselves as well. And to precisely the extent that Durkheim's problems and solutions *were* different from our own, we are confronted with the extraordinary diversity—and thus the sheer, radical contingency—of the ways in which people can, have, and might again think about their societies. To read Durkheim's works, and to read them (in so far as it is possible) in his terms rather then our own, is thus to confront and explore the almost limitless possibilities of the sociological imagination. There is no better—and there may be no other—antidote for the constraints in question.

Bibliography

Bloor, David (1984). "Durkheim and Mauss Revisited: Classification and the Sociology of Knowledge," in N. Stehr and V. Meja (eds), *Society and Knowledge: Contemporary Perspectives in the Sociology of Knowledge*. New Brunswick and London: Transaction Books. Pp. 51–75.

Coser, Lewis A. (1971). *Masters of Sociological Thought*. New York: Harcourt, Brace, Jovanovich.

Durkheim, Emile (1893). *De la division du travail social: étude sur l'organisation des sociétés supérieures*. Paris: Alcan, 1893. Translated by George Simpson as *The Division of Labor in Society*. New York: Free Press, 1933.

———— (1895). *Les Règles de la méthode sociologique*. Paris: Alcan. Edited, with an Introduction, by Steven Lukes, and translated by W.D. Halls, as *The Rules of Sociological Method and Selected Texts on Sociology and Its Method*. New York: Free Press, 1982.

———— (1897a). "Labriola, Antonio, *Essais sur la conception matérialiste de l'histoire*," *Revue philosophique*, XLIV, pp. 645–51. Translated by Mark Traugott as "Revue of Antonio Labriola, *Essais sur la conception matérialiste de l'histoire*," in Mark Traugott (ed.), *Emile Durkheim on Institutional Analysis*. Chicago and London: University of Chicago Press, 1978. Pp. 123–30.

———— (1897b). *Le Suicide: étude de sociologie*. Paris: Alcan. Translated by J.A. Spaulding and G. Simpson as *Suicide: A Study in Sociology*. New York: Free Press, 1951.

———— (1898a). "L'Individualisme et les intellectuels," *Revue bleue*, 4e sèrie X (1898), pp. 7–13. Translated by S. Lukes and J. Lukes as "Individualism and the Intellectuals" in *Political Studies*, Volume XVII (1969), pp. 19–30; reprinted in W.S.F. Pickering (ed.), *Durkheim on Religion*. London: Routledge and Kegan Paul, 1975. Pp. 59–73.

———— (1898b). "La Prohibition de l'inceste et ses origines," *L'Année sociologique*, Vol. I (1898), pp. 1–70. Translated, with an Introduction, by Edward Sagarin as *Incest: The Nature and Origin of the Taboo*. New York: Lyle Stuart, 1963. Pp. 13–119.

———— (1898c). "Représentations individuelles et représentations collectives," *Revue de métaphysique et de morale*, Vol. VI (1898), pp. 273–303. Translated by D.F. Pocock in E. Durkheim, *Sociology and Philosophy*. New York: Free Press, 1974. Pp. 1–34.

———— (1899). "De la définition des phénomènes religieux," *L'Année sociologique*, Vol. II (1899), pp. 1–28. Translated by Jaqueline Redding and W.S.F. Pickering as "Concerning the Definition of Religious Phenomena" in W.S.F. Pickering (ed.), *Durkheim on Religion*. London: Routledge and Kegan Paul, 1975. Pp. 74–99.

159

Durkheim, Emile (1900). "La Sociologie en France au XIXe siècle," *Revue bleue*, 43 sèrie, XII, pp. 609–13, 647–52. Translated by Mark Traugott as "Sociology in France in the Nineteenth Century," in Robert N. Ballah (ed.), *Emile Durkheim on Morality and Society: Selected Writings*. Chicago and London: University of Chicago Press, 1973. Pp. 3–22.

———— (1901). "Préface de la seconde édition," in *Les Règles de la méthode sociologique*, 2nd edition. Paris: Alcan. Translated by W.D. Halls as "Preface to the Second Edition," in E. Durkheim, *The Rules of Sociological Method*. New York: Free Press, 1982. Pp. 34–47.

———— (1902a). "Préface de la seconde édition: Quelques remarques sur les groupements professionels," in *De la division du travail social*, 2nd edition. Paris: Alcan. Translated by George Simpson as "Preface to the Second Edition: Some Notes on Occupational Groups," in E. Durkheim, *The Division of Labor in Society*. New York: Free Press, 1933. Pp. 1–31.

———— (1902b). "Sur le totémisme," *L'Année sociologique*, Vol. V, pp. 82–121. Translated by R.A. Jones as "On Totemism," *History of Sociology*, Vol. I, nos. 1–2 (1985), in press.

———— (1903). "De quelques formes primitives de classification: contribution a l'étude des représentations collectives," *L'Année sociologique*, Vol. VI, pp. 1–72. Translated, with an Introduction, by Rodney Needham as *Primitive Classification*. Chicago: University of Chicago Press, 1963.

———— (1906). "La Détermination du fait moral," *Bulletin de la société française de philosophie*, Vol. VI (Séances du 11 février et du 22 mars). Reproduced, with excerpts from the discussion, in Durkheim, *Sociologie et philosophie*. Paris: Alcan, 1924. Translated by D.F. Pocock, with an Introduction by J.G. Peristiany, as *Sociology and Philosophy*. New York: Free Press, 1974. Pp. 35–79.

———— (1912). *Les Formes élémentaires de la vie religieuse: le système totémique en Australie*. Paris: Alcan. Translated by Joseph Ward Swain as *The Elementary Forms of the Religious Life: A Study in Religious Sociology*. New York: Macmillan, 1915.

———— (1913). "Le Problème religieux et la dualité de la nature humaine," *Bulletin de la société française de philosophie*, Vol. XIII (Séance du 4 février), pp. 63–113. Translated by R.A. Jones and W.P. Vogt as "The Problem of Religion and the Duality of Human Nature" in H. Kuklick and E. Long (eds), *Knowledge and Society: Studies in the Sociology of Culture, Past and Present*, Volume V. Greenwich, Conn.: JAI Press, 1984. Pp. 1–44.

———— (1925). *L'Education morale*. Paris: Alcan. Translated by Everett K. Wilson and Herman Schnurer as *Moral Education: A Study in the Theory and Application of the Sociology of Education*. New York: Free Press, 1961.

———— (1938). *L'Evolution pédagogique en France*. Paris: Presses Universitaires de France. Translated by Peter Collins as *The Evolution of Educational Thought*. London, Henley, and Boston: Routledge and Kegan Paul, 1977.

———— (1955). *Pragmatisme et sociologie*. Paris: Vrin. Translated by J.C. Whitehouse as *Pragmatism and Sociology*. Cambridge: Cambridge University Press, 1983.

Geertz, Clifford (1973). *The Interpretation of Cultures: Selected Essays*. New York: Basic Books.

Lukes, Steven (1972). *Emile Durkheim: His Life and Work: A Historical and Critical Study*. New York: Harper and Row.

Lukes, Steven (1982). "Introduction," in S. Lukes (ed.), *Durkheim: The Rules of Sociological Method and Selected Texts on Sociology and its Method.* New York: Free Press. Pp. 1–27.

—— and Scull, Andrew (1983). "Introduction," in S. Lukes and A. Scull (eds), *Durkheim and the Law.* New York: St Martin's Press. Pp. 1–32.

Needham, Rodney (1963). "Introduction" to *Primitive Classification,* Chicago: University of Chicago Press. Pp. vii–xlviii.

Pickering, W.S.F. (1984). *Durkheim's Sociology of Religion: Themes and Theories.* London: Routledge and Kegan Paul.

Runciman, W.G. (1983). *A Treatise on Social Theory.* Volume I : *The Methodology of Social Theory.* Cambridge: Cambridge University Press.

Seger, Imogen (1957). *Durkheim and His Critics on the Sociology of Religion.* New York: Monograph Series, Bureau of Applied Social Research, Columbia University.

Smith, Adam (1776). *An Inquiry into the Nature and Causes of the Wealth of Nations.* New York: Modern Library, 1937.

Smith, William Robertson (1889). *Lectures on the Religion of the Semites.* First Series: *The Fundamental Institutions.* Edinburgh: A. and C. Black. Second edition, revised and enlarged. London: A. and C. Black, 1894.

Stanner, W.E.H. (1967). "Reflections on Durkheim and Aboriginal Religion," in M. Freedman (ed.), *Social Organization: Essays Presented to Raymond Firth.* Chicago: Aldine. Pp. 217–40.

Index

About the Author

Robert Alun Jones is Associate Professor of Sociology at the University of Illinois, where he also teaches in the Departments of History and Religious Studies. He received his Ph.D. in American Civilization from the University of Pennsylvania in 1969, and has been an editor of *Knowledge and Society: Studies in the Sociology of Culture, Past and Present* (JAI Press). His articles have appeared in the *American Journal of Sociology*, the *Journal of the History of the Behavioral Sciences*, the *Annual Review of Sociology*, and elsewhere. He is currently working on a book on the intellectual context of Durkheim's *Les Formes élémentaires de la vie religieuse*.